AN
ARCHITECT'S GUIDE
TO
ENGINEERED SHADING SOLUTIONS

THE **NEXT GENERATION** IN WINDOW COVERINGS

NEIL PERRY
GORDON

AN ARCHITECT'S GUIDE TO ENGINEERED
SHADING SOLUTIONS
THE NEXT GENERATION IN WINDOW COVERINGS

iUniverse books may be ordered through booksellers or by contacting:

iUniverse
1663 Liberty Drive
Bloomington, IN 47403
www.iuniverse.com
1-800-Authors (1-800-288-4677)

ISBN: 978-1-4917-4475-8 (sc)
ISBN: 978-1-4917-4476-5 (e)

Library of Congress Control Number: 2014916229

Print information available on the last page.

iUniverse rev. date: 04/06/2016

To my parents, Elaine and Walter Gordon. I am truly fortunate, along with my brother and sister, to have two unique and amazing individuals as parents. It's through their confidence in me, which began at an early stage in my life, that I am able to reach this point in my career to write *An Architect's Guide to Engineered Shading Solutions.*

Cover Photo

The cover photo is of the MUSE Museum of Science in Trento, Italy, which was designed by architect Renzo Piano. The exterior shading solution used for this project was the FM41 system, which is manufactured by Model Systems Italia.

Contents

Contents

Foreword

It's been said that the world is getting smaller, and that may be true, but it is also expanding. Communication via the Internet and ease of travel are taking us places that previous generations only dreamed of. We meet people and make new friends, discover new opportunities and possibilities that offer us a chance to look at the world differently, and become inspired to expand our knowledge in directions we never considered before.

One day, nearly fifteen years ago, while enjoying a beautiful sunny afternoon in Cabo San Lucas, thousands of miles from our Alaskan home, my world was getting ready for a big change. The sun was hot, the pool felt great, the drinks were cold, and everyone appeared to be happy.

My wife and I were sipping drinks in the pool when a man floated by and asked, "What's good to drink around here?"

Barbara answered, "We really like the Dirty Monkey."

At that very moment, our lives and our world expanded. We had met Neil Gordon.

Another twist of fate brought me into the window-covering business back in 1985. At that time, I had no idea how far the new business would take me. With the help of many along the way—and much learning from trial and error—I look back with gratitude and amazement on what has transpired during the past thirty years. Neil Gordon has been a friend, a great teacher, and a visionary. Neil is always willing to teach, share, and expand my knowledge.

When I started in 1985, the options for window coverings were just expanding in a way that had not been seen before. Draperies were starting to decline, and blinds and shades were getting ready to make a huge shift in growth. Since then, the options for both exterior and interior window coverings have become more complex. At the same time, they provide many great solutions for issues like energy efficiency, UV control, daylighting, ease of operation, motorization, and decorative and architectural design.

I have been amazed by how Neil Gordon has taken his thirty years of experience in the window-covering business to develop systems and strategies that assist the design and architectural community. With his innovative, cutting-edge ideas, Neil has been an invaluable partner to many designers and architects. He has educated them about the latest window-covering options and assisted them with concept, design, and installation.

I look forward to the future in our industry. Motorization is becoming the standard, and energy efficiency and sustainable building are the driving forces in every facet of design and building. We are in exciting times. I am sure Neil Gordon will be working tirelessly and passionately to present the newest concepts from around the world. His designs will become the future standards.

It has been a pleasure to have my world expanded by Neil Gordon for the past fifteen years after our chance meeting. I am so grateful to have a friend and business associate who has shared so much knowledge and vision with so many window-covering providers, designers, and architects. I trust that you will have your world expanded and enriched by Neil's knowledge and his quest for innovative, sustainable solutions for today's design and architectural community.

The world is expanding, and the next generation of window coverings has arrived. Come explore the new world, meet new friends, and try the Dirty Monkey if you get a chance.

Tom Miller
Mini Blind King

Introduction

Why do architects need a guide to engineered shading solutions? Because many in the architectural community view window coverings as an afterthought, and as a result, they may not give their projects the best chances for success. This guide's purpose is to educate professionals in the growing field of engineered shading solutions. As the reader will learn, window coverings have matured way beyond mere decoration and have become a significant part of today's sustainable building systems.

I have been in the window-covering industry my entire life. Starting out as a child, working in my parent's housewares stores, I witnessed an industry grow from simple roller shades to being integrated into today's most sophisticated building facades in the world. I remember that at ten years old I was cutting to size stock roller shades for customers while they watched. I was excited the first time I saw the Levolor Mini Blind introduced in the 1970s. And I was thrilled at the vertical blinds a few years later. I was blown away when Hunter Douglas hit the scene with products in the eighties and nineties, which included Duette and Silhouette shades.

Of course, the history of window coverings protecting us with shading devices from heat, light, and glare goes back much further than the products I grew up with. In the chapter on history, there's a glimpse back to the times of the Romans with their advanced shading systems, the venetian blind, and the evolution of the roller shade.

Today's emphasis on sustainable solutions has rushed window coverings onto center stage with other building systems, such as lighting and HVAC. Architects are becoming aware of the advantages of incorporating window coverings into their building facades.

Additionally, with the emergence of passive-house design in this country, exterior window shading is becoming an important element to consider in order to achieve the passive-house certification. This guide will enable the reader to understand what window coverings provide in terms of heat, light, and glare control for all types of interior environments. With the accelerated maturation of the window-covering industry, we have coined the term *engineered shading solutions*, which defines solutions as more than just throwing a shade on a window.

My goal is to provide an advanced understanding of the evolution of the window-covering industry and the importance of choosing the right engineered shading solution.

Some Extra Words about the Second Edition

It has been more than a year since the first edition of this book was published. During that time, I interviewed six more interesting professionals. I asked these qualified individuals to relate their life's work to my world of engineered shading solutions. The lineup comes from a common yet diverse set of disciplines ranging from architect to researcher to innovator to fabricator to builder to designer. The interviews make for interesting and enlightening reading.

In addition to the interviews, I have added four new chapters: "The Zip Shade," "Shading for the Landscape Architect," "Shading for the Passive House," and "Four Myths about Exterior Window Shades." It is my hope that you find the interviews and the new chapters worthwhile and educational.

Interview with Renato Borsato, CEO Model System Italia

In my many years in the industry I have met inspiring people and companies. At the top of my list is the man I met when I traveled to Treviso, Italy. Renato Borsato is the CEO of Model System Italia. His company creates the most incredible engineered shading solutions I have ever encountered. Below is the interview I conducted with him during one of my visits.

NG: What is the history of Model System?

RB: Model System is a multigenerational family business, founded in 1964 by my father, Egidio Borsato, and my uncle Leopoldo Borsato. My father has since passed away, but my uncle still heads our company. My brother Stefano is the engineering manager, and Leopoldo's two sons Flavio and Roberto are very involved in the business. Flavio is the production manager, and Roberto is the manager of domestic markets.

When my father and uncle started the business fifty years ago, we primarily manufactured venetian blinds (the Model System factory is thirty minutes from Venice). Today, we have grown to more than one hundred employees and produce both interior and exterior shading solutions, serving top architects and contractors throughout the continent and beyond.

NG: How have you seen solar shading evolve in Europe over the past five years?

RB: The evolution of the solar shade has centered on the need to optimize resources and in particular maximize our energy usage. With the extreme high cost of heating and cooling throughout Europe, owners and architects are constantly seeking ways to improve building efficiencies. This evolution has paved the way for innovations such as the double-skin facade on building envelopes throughout Europe. Our blinds and shades have become an integral component of these double-glass building systems. In Europe, and in particular France, these products must meet certain performance standards, and the Model System solutions are leading the way in such compliances.

NG: Many Model System solutions are integrated into the facades of buildings. Whom do you partner with to design such advanced shading systems?

RB: This is an interesting question. We actually need to work with a variety of partners. As our products directly contribute to sustainable solutions, we work with such organizations as the Department of

Construction and Architecture, the Division of Energy and Building Design, and the curtain wall manufacturers. In fact, the curtain wall manufacturers have become an important partner to Model System since we need to work very closely together on projects. Our blinds are designed and manufactured for their integration into facade systems; therefore, the product engineering needs to be coordinated.

NG: What are the most exciting projects you have done?

RB: Model System has participated on some amazing projects, which—thanks to good fortune and strong relationships—were brought to us from several of the world's great architects. For example, we have had a close and long working relationship with Renzo Piano. We recently completed the MUSE complex designed by the Renzo Piano Building Workshop, which is a tremendous opportunity to feature our exterior shading solutions the FM41 and FM51. We also had the pleasure of working with architect Zaha Hadid, the first woman to receive the Pritzker Architecture Prize. We worked with her firm on the Maxxi Museum of Twenty-First Century Arts in Rome and the Hotel Silken Puerta America in Madrid.

Another exciting project we were specified on is the Zurich Insurance Headquarters in Milan. The architect Alessandro Scandurra featured our FM51 system across the entire facade, and our shades have become a key visual element of the building.

Model System is able to provide shading solutions globally. You can find our systems throughout Italy, France, Switzerland, Luxemburg, Portugal, Spain, and Greece. In addition, we will soon have a presence in North and South America.

NG: What do you see as the future of engineered shading solutions?

RB: At Model System, we are engineering and developing products that meet the demanding needs of tomorrow's dynamic facades. Our fabrication capabilities are second to none in the industry. Architects know if they can design it, we can build it. With this in mind, I see the future of engineered shading solutions as a growing, integrated building system that architects cannot ignore. The shading solutions we provide can meet the needs of energy-efficient buildings and provide comfort to occupants from small residential projects to large commercial complexes.

Chapter 1

Definition of Engineered Shading Solutions

For the past several years, my business has focused on serving the architectural community. One of my primary ways of reaching architects has been by providing health, safety, and welfare continuing education credits for my popular Lunch and Learn programs. These hour-long presentations introduces the concept of engineered shading solutions to the architectural community.

Through the hundreds of presentations I have done, I have taught many architects, designers, and specifiers about the world of window coverings. In the process, I have shared that window coverings are no longer the simple devices of the past—they have evolved into an integrated strategy for today's sustainable buildings and interiors. Therefore, a more comprehensive description was needed, and the term *engineered shading solutions* was coined.

As a building system, engineered shading solutions are more than just a quick fix of installing basic shades and expecting superior performance. In order to successfully control solar heat gain, glare caused by daylighting, and the levels of light in a space, engineered shading solutions need to be part of the initial planning and design stages of building facades.

With such high expectations comes my definition:

> Engineered shading solutions are sustainable systems
> for interior and exterior window coverings, which

engage the latest technologies to control heat, glare, and light.

Engineered shading solutions contribute ideas, products, and results for sustainable architecture. *Engineered* means a creative application of scientific principles to design and develop structures with respect to their intended functions. *Shading solutions* refers to the answers to common issues and problems caused by too much solar heat gain, glare, and light. Combined, architects can achieve successful results in providing for the health, safety, and welfare of the occupants of their designs.

The premise of this book is to dig deeper into the definition of engineered shading solutions. What does it mean to be called a *sustainable system*? How does a system—for interior and exterior various applications—actually provide solutions for excessive solar heat gain and annoying glare while regulating the amount of light into a space?

Chapter 2

History of Popular Shading Solutions

Engineered shading solutions have an interesting history that can be traced back thousands of years. The Greeks and Romans built porticos to provide shade from the elements, and many of these static structures can still be admired throughout historic sites in many European cities. While the porticos were effective, they had no moving parts, which is a key aspect of an engineered shading solution. However, a few of today's popular shading solutions that meet our definition of engineered shading solutions originated in earlier times: roman shades, venetian blinds, and roller shades.

The Roman Shade

In the heyday of the Roman Colosseum (AD 70-80), crowds were entertained with spectacular gladiator contests in the open air. To protect the spectators from the harsh Italian sun, awnings were constructed that partially covered the arena and offered sun protection. The awnings were an elaborate system of ropes and pulleys called the velarium. *Velarium* was the Latin name given for this retractable awning system in the Roman Colosseum.

When they were not in use, the shades folded back on themselves, much like the modern shading style—the roman shade. What a feat of innovation and success that even in AD 70-80, they were able to effectively reduce solar heat issues while creating a truly beautiful engineered shading solution.

Source: http://www.tribunesandtriumphs.org/colosseum/awning-at-the-colosseum.htm

The Velarium

The Venetian Blind

The early Venetians were great traders, and they are thought to have taken the idea of the venetian blind from Persia to Venice. The Venetian slaves, once freed, are believed to have brought the blind to France as a means of their livelihood. The first proof of blinds in America was in 1761 at St. Peter's Church in Philadelphia where the windows were fitted with venetian blinds.

The first entrepreneur of the venetian blind, John Webster of London, advertised his wares in 1767. Venetian blinds then appeared in the 1787 painting by J. L. Gerome Ferris, entitled *The Visit of Paul Jones to the Constitutional Convention.*

Other illustrations show venetian blinds at Independence Hall in Philadelphia at the time of the signing of the Declaration of Independence. The first large modern building in the United States

to adopt venetian blinds was Rockefeller Center's RCA Building in New York City at the turn of the twentieth century.
Source: http://www.mae.ncsu.edu/silverberg/AdaptiveShading/history.htm

Tea by James Tissot, 1872

History of the Roller Shade

The Scotch Holland Roller Blinds originated in the early 1700s. They were made from Holland linen, which came from the Netherlands. The fabric was first produced in Glasgow, Scotland, by James Louis Robertson and John King, hence the name Scotch Holland. The first roller shade made from Scotch Holland linen did not have a spring mechanism. Instead, when the blind was closed, the fabric lay in folds on the windowsill. To open the blind, you had to pull on a cord that was attached to a top rod. To secure the open blind, you wound the cord around a cleat.

In 1864, Stewart Hartshorn patented the first spring roller design using a ratchet and gravity pawl. This spring roller window shade was the forerunner of today's roller shades, and it used a spring mechanism to allow fabric to be rolled up or down. The spring roller window shade became very popular in America, and several production plants were opened in the early twentieth century. Below is a drawing of the spring roller, and below that is the crank Star Shade cutting machine from the 1920s.

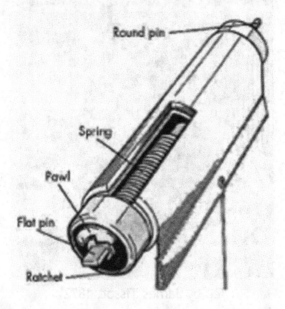

Spring Roller Star Shade Cutting Machine

Chapter 3

Sustainable Design

Engineered shading solutions are sustainable systems for interior and exterior window coverings, which engage the latest technologies to control heat, glare, and light.

As previously defined, we should now understand the concept of engineered shading solutions. However, there is much more to this definition that needs explaining. The following chapters will further define what it means for a shading solution to be a *sustainable* system. What are the interior and exterior solutions that can actually control heat, light, and glare? How do these systems function?

Let's start with the concept of sustainable design. According to the American Institute of Architects (AIA), the definition of a sustainable design is:

> Sustainable design is a collaborative process that involves thinking ecologically—studying systems, relationships, and interactions in order to design in ways that remove rather than contribute stress from systems.
> Source:http://www.aia.org/education/ces/AIAB089084

There are countless situations of poorly designed window covering solutions that actually add stress to systems. A common example is when floor-length draperies block heating units and trap the warm air. However, when done correctly, engineered shading solutions successfully reduce stress from building systems.

A great example is from architect Roger Bayley. He specified automated exterior solar shades to reduce solar heat gain in the rooms of the Vancouver Olympic Village, which reduced the stress of that system in order for the radiant cooling and heating system to function properly. The interview with Roger is included in the chapter "Exterior Shading Solutions."

The US Green Building Council

The US Green Building Council (USGBC) is a nonprofit organization that promotes sustainability in how buildings are designed, built, and operated. USGBC is best known for its development of the Leadership in Energy and Environmental Design (LEED). The LEED program is a third-party verification of green buildings.

The USGBC guidelines for LEED designation provide examples of how engineered shading solutions can remove stress from systems. Additionally, the following LEED strategies illuminate how window coverings perform at equivalent levels as other sophisticated building systems. While there are many ways to earn LEED points, the following strategies are the most enlightening: daylighting, light pollution reduction, energy reduction, and recycled content.

Daylighting

Harvesting of natural daylight into a space is a priority of modern design. However, the most common failure of this strategy is the glare caused by excessive light levels. Therefore, glare control is required, and the USGBC recommends shades to remedy this stress. Engineered shading solutions can provide the technology to reduce glare by as much as 95 percent with high-performance fabrics. The chapter "Fabric Technologies" describes more about glare control.

Light Pollution Reduction

For projects to earn points for light pollution reduction, the USGBC requires that windows must have shades that are motorized and timed, thereby reducing the environmental stress caused by nighttime light spilling into the surrounding neighborhood. These automated systems are discussed in the chapter "Smart Control."

Energy Reduction

The reduction of solar energy entering a space and reducing the amount of energy used for cooling is where engineered shading solutions perform best. Exterior solar shades can reduce solar heat gain by as much as 85 percent. Further energy reduction solutions are discussed in several areas of this book.

Recycled Content

The USGBC states, "There is an increase in demand for building products that incorporate recycled materials, thereby reducing impacts resulting from extraction and processing of virgin materials." Source: http://www.kone.us/sustainability/leed/

GreenScreen Revive is a revolutionary new sustainable window shade fabric. GreenScreen Revive combines sustainable values with outstanding performance and has been Cradle-to-Cradle Certified. The Cradle-to-Cradle Certified program, founded by William McDonough and Dr. Michael Braungart, is a third-party program that assesses a product's safety to humans and the environment and design for future life cycles.

GreenScreen Revive offers excellent solar control, reduces heat and glare, and offers a remarkably clean view to the outdoors (owing to its finely knitted weaves). This fire-retardant, PVC-free fabric is constructed of 100 percent polyester yarn and a minimum of 89 percent Repreve polyester. Repreve is recycled and recyclable, contains low VOCs, and is made in the USA. To help visualize how well the Repreve fabric works as a sustainable product, we can determine that twelve sixteen-ounce water bottles can effectively produce enough yarn to weave one yard of fabric. Source: http://www.draperinc.com/WindowShades/revive.asp

Interview with Darren Macri of Bleu Nest Builders

The news about Cornell Tech on Roosevelt Island in New York City has been very exciting to those who follow passive-house trends. Handel Architects have designed the tallest passive-house building in the world. This high-rise dormitory building with its energy efficiency will change the way buildings are constructed though out the USA.

Closer to my neck of the woods, in Ramsey, New Jersey, Darren Macri is building a smaller but still significant passive-house project. The local builder specializes in passive-house technology and systems. We discussed a few things about the passive-house concepts and how exterior solar shades are a part of the solution to energy efficiencies.

NG: Where did the concept of passive homes come from?

DM: Going back thousands of years, native people have known the benefits of the low winter sun and heating their south-facing homes. The Sinagua people of Arizona would only build in caves that faced south and had long overhangs to block the high summer sun—the first exterior shading device!

The idea of making modern homes more efficient and more comfortable actually began in the 1970s in North America. But when oil prices dropped in 1985, the efficient home movement in North America died. In Germany, a physicist named Dr. Wolfgang Feist put together the best ideas that we left behind. He reworked those ideas to create one cohesive approach, and as Germans like to do, he put metrics to it and built home-energy-modeling software. It became predictable and measurable. He wanted to find the sweet spot where you can make the house efficient enough to eliminate the large central HVAC units. Then you can take that saving and put it toward windows and insulation. He built the first passive house in Darmstadt, Germany, in 1999.

NG: How did you get started with passive homes?

DM: I am a LEED AP, and while there are some very nice things about LEED, I felt that it needed to be more aggressive in tackling energy issues. I discovered passive house at a conference, and I thought, *Hey, beautiful, where have you been all my life?*

NG: Tell me about the project in Ramsey.

DM: We are building New Jersey's very first certified passive house. Our home will use up to 90 percent less heating and cooling energy than a standard constructed home—we can heat the house with the power of a hair dryer. While the energy savings are good, the best part of a passive house is the comfort. The nice, evenly tempered rooms stay rock steady no matter what is happening outside, and perfect humidity—never too dry in the winter—leads to super-high indoor air quality.

NG: What is the future of the passive house?

DM: The future of passive house is happening around us right now. It is exploding in a major way. New York City just announced the world's tallest passive house, which will be built on Roosevelt Island. Since January of 2015, every new building in Brussels has to be built to the passive-house standard. A bill that is making its way through city hall will mandate that all new municipal buildings be built to this standard. People and nations all over are realizing that passive house doesn't cost much more up front, is more comfortable and healthier, and is great for the environment.

NG: How do exterior window shades fit into the passive house?

DM: Exterior shading is essential for most passive-house projects. Ideally, most of your south-facing walls would be 20 percent glazing. You want that low winter sun to heat up the house, but you have to block that high summer sun before it gets in. If you don't, your battle is lost, which will lead to overheating. For the west and east windows, that short direct sun can really be complicated and also can lead to overheating. Exterior shading is the best way to combat that.

Chapter 4

The Dynamic Facade

Since the advent of man seeking shelter, the concept of the third skin has been critical to survival. Human skin is the first skin, clothing is the second skin, and the facades of our buildings are the third skin. The third skin describes the intimate relationship between humans and living spaces. Today, the concept of the third skin has evolved into the popular designation of the *dynamic facade*.

The dynamic facade is the filter between the indoor and outdoor environments. This filter should provide protection from the elements (such as heat and cold), an exchange of ventilated fresh air, sufficient natural daylight, and a connection with the outdoors. A significant player within the structure of the dynamic facade is engineered shading solutions. The diagram below shows how window coverings are integrated along with other building systems such as HVAC and lighting.

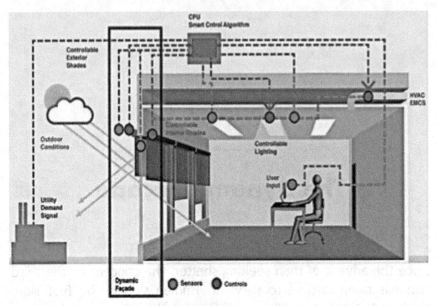

The Dynamic Facade

Living or working in a building with too much solar heat gain, glare, or light can provide intense discomfort to the occupants. These issues are usually the main concerns clients have when we are brought in to the project. It is proven that thermal and visual comfort have beneficial effects on the occupants' well-being. That is why today's sustainable buildings are incorporating the concept of the dynamic facade. Engineered shading solutions, along with other systems of the dynamic facade, provide the necessary stress-reducing results that static systems cannot offer.

Heating, cooling, and lighting constitute 57 percent of total energy usage in commercial buildings, and facades have a large influence over these loads. An advanced management utilization of natural energy sources, such as sunshine, daylight, and external air, can significantly reduce this figure. An automated engineered shading solution is one example of the variety of methods available. Switching to an automated shading system can save between 20 and 40 percent of energy used—while only accounting for about 2 percent of the total building costs.

Engineered shading solutions are at the frontier of the exciting field of the dynamic facade. Subsequent chapters provide specific details about the various automated systems that contribute to the performance of today's building envelopes.

To further enhance the topic of the dynamic facade, we conducted several interviews. The transcripts are presented below. The first one is with Stephan Selkowitz, the group leader of the Windows and Envelope Materials Group for Lawrence Berkeley National Laboratory.

Interview with Stephen Selkowitz of Berkeley National Laboratory

Stephen Selkowitz is the group leader of the Windows and Envelope Materials Group for Lawrence Berkeley National Laboratory. Berkeley Lab is a member of the national laboratory system, which is supported by the US Department of Energy and is managed by the University of California. Stephen is an internationally recognized expert on window technologies, facade systems, and daylighting.

NG: Why does the Lawrence Berkeley National Laboratory study high-performance building facade solutions?

SS: In the US, buildings alone constitute 39 percent of all energy usage. And remarkably, commercial buildings' energy usage is about half of that percentage. That's 18 percent of the total energy used in the United States.

NG: I understand that one of Berkeley Lab's missions is to assist industries to bring sustainable engineered shading solutions to market. How is this done?

SS: First, we work with manufacturers to help them develop dynamic shading products through our test facilities. We can advise on improved materials and controls. We assist architects and engineers to measure and optimize performance of various solutions, and we collaborate with contractors and owners to measure and document field performance.

NG: What technology has Berkeley Labs developed?

SS: Sometimes, we develop our own technology that we license out to industry, such as window sensors that send signals via Wi-Fi to control shades based on the weather conditions. We have also worked with manufacturers, such as Pella, in developing an in-between glass motorized shade.

NG: As a function of the dynamic facade, how do we understand the cost benefit of installing engineered shading solutions?

SS: One of the missing links of calculating the cost benefit is the investment in the comfort of the occupants. This measurement of productivity through comfort may be the driving force—not energy payback.

NG: What is your recommendation for an engineered shading solution: a solar shade or a horizontal louver?

SS: Most times, that depends on the owner's aesthetics. Louvers provide some daylighting advantages by bouncing the light off the louvers into the space, while shades can disappear from view. A clever solution is a combination of splitting the facade treatment into two components. The top section of the engineered shading solution harvests daylight with louvers, and the bottom part reduces glare with a solar shade.

NG: What considerations go into choosing between an interior shading solution and an exterior shading solution?

SS: Many times, that decision depends on the performance of the glass and the local climate. High-performance glazing can function fine with interior shades in cooler climates. Meanwhile, lower-quality glazing may require exterior shades to lower solar heat gain. In some instances, both are necessary: interior shades for glare control and exterior shades to control solar heat gain.

Interview with Tali Mejicovsky of Arup Architects

During a recent presentation I gave at the architectural and engineering firm Arup, a leader in facade design, I had the pleasure to sit down with Tali Mejicovsky, a facade engineer to discuss the roll of building envelopes and exterior shading solutions.

NG: What does the facade team at Arup do?

TM: Arup provides specialist advice on all aspects of building facades. Our aim is to assist our clients in realizing their objectives for appearance, performance, durability, quality, cost, and schedule. We seek to optimize facade solutions for our clients on every project. Our facade group is part of the worldwide Arup. We are a networked business based in New York, Los Angeles, and San Francisco. We have fifteen other international offices.

Our international team is more than 150 strong. From this broad base, we deploy our resources effectively to meet demands, whether it is a tight schedule or a requirement for specific areas of expertise. Arup undertakes design work for architects, project managers, developers, and subcontractors, and we also have extensive experience in building diagnostics and remediation for a wide range of building owners. Typically accounting for around 15 percent of a building's construction cost—the same as the structure—a facade is an important consideration for any project. Arup provides impartial advice to owners and managers to help them manage the technical, commercial, and program risks associated with facade and roof elements.

Our expertise encompasses an extensive range of materials and systems, including curtain wall consultancy, building physics assessment, daylight management and glare control, energy and building envelope performance optimization, forensics and remedial, microclimate weather analysis, and parametric modeling. Arup's design, technical, and commercial expertise helps achieve the key to the success of building projects down to the smallest detail.

NG: What is your role?

TM: I am an associate within Arup New York's facades group. As a senior person, my role is to win work, mentor the younger facade engineers, and provide technical advice on projects. I also project manage facade projects and work to grow the group and our business.

NG: How has designing facades changed over the years?

TM: During my career, the fashion in facades has changed from designing cable-supported facades to framed glazing with larger and larger sizes. There is a trend toward eliminating the framing as much as possible, both to increase daylight openings and reduce frame effects on lowering the U-value, but mostly from an aesthetic point of view. Increasingly we are seeing all-glass facades with minimal metal connectors laminated into the glass thickness, thereby hiding all structural connections. At the same time, there is also an increased understanding of the facade's contribution to energy savings and code-mandated thermal and solar criteria that the facade must meet. This driver is mediating the desire to go to an all-glass facade.

NG: How have engineered shading solutions become an integral part of today's facades?

TM: In order to efficiently address energy savings and occupant comfort, shading solutions are employed. This is not a new phenomenon, particularly in very hot climates where screens have traditionally been an architectural solution to mitigate the sun. Depending on the architect's aesthetic, the shading solutions may be internal, external, fabric, metal, or glass.

NG: Can you tell me some of the projects you have done or are working on now that include window coverings?

TM: Current and recent project with exterior window coverings include:

- Northeastern Interdisciplinary Science and Engineering Building features exterior shading including vertical curved aluminum fins and horizontal aluminum tubes.
- Harvard Art Museum features an exterior glazed louver system.
- Duke University LSRC Annex incorporates horizontal sunshades and louvers and vertical fins.
- Frick Chemistry Building at Princeton University uses cast aluminum sunshades as exterior shading.
- Sheraton Hotel at New Songdo City in Korea incorporated perforated metal sheet exterior sunshades as a 45-degree angle to the glazing.
- Aurora Place, Sydney, Australia: eighteen-story residential Macquarie Apartments. Units feature a fully operable glass-louvered east facade at the generous three-meter-deep apartment balconies.
- Walsh Bay in Sydney, Australia, features exterior operable louver frames to open and close balcony spaces.
- Project Rodeo, BP Westlake in Houston features custom horizontal sunshades designed to shield the occupants from solar radiation while allowing daylight throughout double-story trading and support spaces. Building was certified LEED Platinum.

NG: Where do you see facade design going in the buildings of the future?

TM: Facades are striving to become more adaptable to changing conditions with phase-changing materials, electro-chromic, photo-chromic, and gas-chromic materials. Sunshades that open and close or rotate in response to the sun will be implemented more often. Facades that create energy (photovoltaic, bio-algae facade) will be readily available. Changing facades are likely to be designed on the buildings of the future.

Interview with Gianni Stramandinoli of Stahlbau Pichler

There is a revolution brewing. Never in the past thirty years that I have been in the industry have I seen such radical new products that are about to shake up the world of window coverings. No longer will we see shades and blinds only as interior solutions. Window coverings are becoming the "fourth skin" in architecture—skin is the first, clothing is the second, third is the building envelope, and the fourth is an exterior shading solution to protect the building itself.

This dramatic move to the exterior is happening with exciting new products from Europe, and from Italy in particular. Last summer, while visiting Model System Italia, a manufacturer of incredible shading systems, I had the pleasure of touring the manufacturing facility of Stahlbau Pichler, a provider of building facades worldwide. I saw the marriage between the envelopes of buildings and window coverings (the fourth skin).

Below is my interview with Gianni Stramandinoli, the key account manager for Stahlbau Pichler in the USA.

NG: Tell me about the history of Stahlbau Pichler.

GS: For decades now, Stahlbau Pichler has been planning, producing, delivering, and erecting steel structures and facades for buildings on an international scale. We undertake every aspect of project management, thus improving quality while reducing time and costs.

Today, with more than two hundred employees and a track record of more than 2,500 contracts completed, we can manage every phase of a project from the initial feasibility study to final construction, drawing on an annual production capacity of 25,000 tons of steel and 70,000 m² of curtain wall.

Our concept is a symbiosis of Italian design and German precision. Headquartered in Bolzano, we also have offices in Milan, Germany, Switzerland, Russia, and Austria. Our core skills are in the realization of buildings used for industrial, commercial, and administration purposes, bridge construction, protective buildings, and traffic engineering. Architects such as David Chipperfield, Sauerbruch &

Hutton, Massimiliano Fuksas, Norman Foster, Zaha Hadid, and Kenzo Tange are all appreciating and making use of our know-how.

NG: Are you currently working on projects in the USA?

GS: We have done several buildings in New York over the past several years. Our current project is at 520 West Twenty-Eighth Street, next to the High Line. It's a beautifully designed facade, designed by the internationally renowned architect Zaha Hadid.

NG: How have the building envelope and facades changed over the years?

GS: Building envelopes and facades become more innovative, energy-efficient, and integrative. This is seen with the technological advances in glass. We have many commercial buildings throughout Europe that use the "double-skin" concept, which are two layers of glass forming the building envelope and typically installed with blinds in between.

NG: Why is it important to integrate window coverings into the facade during manufacturing?

GS: Architects are designing buildings with exterior window coverings as part of the facade. This may be a blind within the double skin or shades exposed on the outer walls. Either way, these are not afterthoughts and need to be designed by the architect so they are integrated into the facades we produce. We may be simply pre-mounting installation brackets or creating pockets for the shades.

NG: Describe some projects you have done where shades and blinds are integrated into facades.

GS: There are two projects we have recently completed in Switzerland that show two versions of window coverings. The first one is the Residence Du Parc in Nyon, where the blinds are exposed to the outside of the facade. Wind sensors are required to raise the blinds when conditions warrant. The second is the Maison de la Paix in Geneva, a beautifully designed building showcasing the glass facade with horizontal aluminum blinds within the double skin.

NG: How do you envision the future between building facades and engineered shading solutions?

GS: We are convinced, that the demand for integrated building facades and engineered shading solutions will increase. There have been great advances in curtain-wall technologies. Buildings today and in the future will be constructed with more glass and less visible structural support. This increases the need for effective window coverings to reduce solar heat gain, and with all this natural daylight flooding into the open space, a need to effectively control glare.

Chapter 5

Interior Shading Solutions

The most widely specified window coverings products are *interior shading solutions.* The goal of any engineered shading solution is to reduce stressful conditions, such as solar heat gain, too much light, and/or glare for occupants. Projects and circumstances are never the same, and typically they require a unique, custom-engineered shading solution (depending on the type of installation, such as residential, hospitality, commercial, educational, or health care).

Residential and Hospitality

Although window coverings are as old as antiquity itself, providing engineered shading solutions for the residential and hospitality market is a brand-new frontier. Let's revisit the description of engineered shading solutions:

> Engineered shading solutions are sustainable systems for interior and exterior window coverings, which engage the latest technologies to control heat, glare, and light.

The basic requirement of any occupant of a residence or a guest in a hotel is comfort. Engineered shading solutions can address such comfort issues as solar heat gain, glare, and light.

Another important element for owners in this market—who in some cases, such as with hotels, may not be the occupants—is energy efficiency.

Residential and Hospitality Strategies

Planning for engineered shading solutions in a residence and in guest rooms presents an assortment of unique and common challenges. They include controlling solar heat gain, reducing glare, blocking UV rays, regulating sunlight, and automating and integrating the systems.

Solar Heat Gain

In a residence or a guest room, engineered shading solutions are designed to reduce solar heat gain in the summer months and reduce heat loss in the winter months, both with the intention of reducing energy costs.

Summer strategies for engineered shading solutions include specifying high-performance fabrics to reflect as much as 50 percent of the solar heat gain. Details about these fabrics are included in the chapter "Fabric Technologies." For the high-end residential and hospitality markets, automation is now widely used with weather stations tracking the sun across the sky and positioning the shades to provide the best protection. Automation is also discussed in the chapter "Smart Controls."

During the winter months, engineered shading solutions can be designed to be used as insulators. These treatments are those that trap air, such as cellular shades or double-lined draperies. The R-value is what measures the solution's performance. The R-value is the capacity of an insulating material to resist heat flow. The higher the R-value, the greater its insulating power.

Glare Control

The number one complaint for glare control in the home or guest room is usually on the TV or computer screen. This may happen when direct light or a reflection of light makes it difficult to see the screen. The most effective way to significantly reduce glare is with darker color solar shade fabric. The chapter "Fabric Technologies" explains in detail how these fabrics work.

UV Control

The ultraviolet (UV) rays of the sun can destroy expensive finishes and fabrics. UV rays will cause colors on fabrics to fade because the energy starts a chemical reaction in the molecules. The chemical reaction causes the molecules to become different molecules, resulting in a fading of the color. To protect an interior from the harmful UV rays, solar shade fabric with a tight weave is required. This is known as the "openness" and is explained in the chapter "Fabric Technologies."

Light Control

The highest demand for light control is in the bedroom as well as in hotel guest rooms. Many people like a dark room on demand and some need pitch-blackness in order to sleep. This is best accomplished with blackout fabrics and side channels, both of which are detailed in chapters to come.

Automation

Automation in a residence or a guest room may be as simple as a remote control to raise or lower the shades, or it may be integrated with other systems, such as lights and media. All types of motorization and automation are discussed in the chapter "Smart Controls."

Commercial and Educational

Engineered shading solutions are being recognized around the world for improving productivity for businesses and increased grades for students as well as overall improved ability and motivation. According to Judith Heerwagen, a former scientist with the Pacific Northwest Laboratory who is now a program expert with the General Services Administration, productivity and the workplace are related in these ways:

- "A building can positively affect ability by providing comfortable ambient conditions, by enabling individual control and adjustment of conditions."
- "A building can positively affect motivation by providing conditions that promote positive affective functioning engagement and personal control. Moods create the 'affective context' for thought processes and behaviors and are directly tied to motivation."
Source: http://www.wbdg.org/resources/psychspace_value.php

Solar Heat Gain

Many office spaces and schools have large open areas with spans of windows from wall to wall and from ceiling to floor. The largest challenge is the control of solar heat gain. Solar shades have become popular among occupants who prefer the ability to see through the fabric while reducing solar heat gain into the space.

Glare Control

The concept of bringing natural light into a space has tremendous benefits for the comfort and performance of the occupants. Interior shading solutions harvest natural daylight by bouncing the light off horizontal louvers into a space, and they also reduce glare significantly with fabric technologies.

Below is an interior daylighting solution that employs 3½-inch aluminum louvers as a light shelf to bounce the light deep into the space, while the lower portion houses a solar shade with high-performing fabric that reduces the glare caused by the harvesting of the natural daylight.

Light Control

Controlling the light in an office or classroom is critical for presentations. Sometimes a blackout condition is required, and the best way to achieve that is with blackout shade cloth and side channels. Further details on this are provided in "Fabric Technologies," "Blackout Shading Solutions," and "Dual Shading Solutions."

Noise Reduction

In spaces with large expanses of windows, sound bouncing off the glass becomes an issue. Engineered shading solutions can reduce this stress with treatments that lower the reflection of sound. The graphic below shows that perfect reflection of sound off glass is 0.0, and perfection absorption is 1.0. These numbers refer to what's known as the *noise reduction coefficient.*

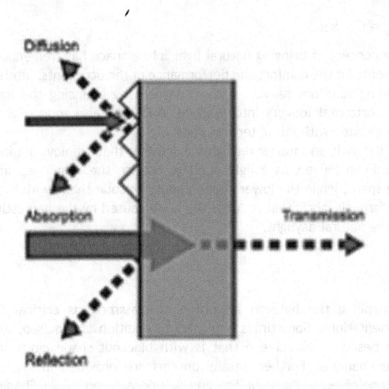

In a recording studio in New York City, solar shades were installed as specified by the acoustical architects Walters-Stork Design Group. Solar shades as tested by Phifer SheerWeave show that the basic 3 percent open weave has an NRC rating of .60.

Automation

Automation for commercial or educational facilities may require complete integration with a building management system or on a smaller scale for presentations in a classroom. Smart control systems are utilized when simultaneous control of shading and lighting is required, which is discussed in detail in the chapter "Smart Controls."

Health Care

Health care facilities have unique needs that only engineered shading solutions can provide. These needs are:

- The reduction of solar heat gain is essential for the comfort of the occupants and also reduces energy costs.
- Glare control is critical when dealing with medical equipment and display screens.
- Harvesting natural daylight over artificial daylight proves beneficial for patients since it encourages well-being and a speedy recovery.
- Utilizing a Dual Shading Solution, which is a combination of both privacy and blackout fabrics, provides the patient with options.
- To provide accessible shading controls to the patients and override control for the nursing staff.

Design

Regardless of the type of installation—residential, hospitality, commercial, education, or health care—once function has been determined, the design decisions come into play (function before form). Engineered shading solutions need to perform as intended, but that doesn't prevent attractive design features. The products shown in this book are all Italian-designed hardware and fabrics with a focus on solar shades and horizontal louver blinds.

Let's look at the design options for the top treatment. The top treatment is the roller, the brackets, and the optional closure devices. There are three types of top treatments: the open roll, the cassette, and the recessed pocket.

Open Roll

The open roll describes the solar shade that displays an exposed roller and mounting brackets. Below is a photo of a typical open roll solution.

The visible brackets and the clutch mechanism are very unattractive and clearly need improvement if they are to be exposed. Another option for the open roll is to use the shade bar with bracket covers as shown below.

Open Roll Design

The open roll is a great solution for tight fits with its sleek and narrow design along with manual controls. For motorized solutions, the exposed roller is not the recommended choice because of the exposed power whip coming from the motor.

Sometimes it is necessary to do a *reverse roll*. That is when the shade cloth falls over the front of the roller, giving extra distance between the glass and the cloth. This is useful if there are window obstructions, such as handles, that need to be cleared. The open roll is available as a regular roll or a reverse roll (as seen in the diagram below).

ROLL STYLE

REGULAR ROLL   **REVERSE ROLL**

Cassettes

Cassettes are an aluminum housing system for the shade roller, fabric, brackets, and controls for both manual and motorized shades. The cassette works well for motorized shades because the power connection can be hidden in the enclosure. Many manufacturers offer different shapes, sizes, and finishes as well as custom finishes. Shown below are two Italian designs with a selection of square or bullnose.

The square design aluminum cassette comes in three sizes and five finishes. The size of any of the cassettes will increase in size along with the roller diameter due to wider widths and/or longer lengths.

Square Cassette

The bullnose cassette is a compact design and comes in three sizes and six finishes.

Bullnose Cassette

Secure Installation

Here is a final comment on cassettes. Shades installed with "end brackets" alone are not as securely installed as cassette-enclosed shades. It is not unusual to find a forty-pound-plus shade installed with only tiny end brackets holding it up. This is an accident waiting to happen. The cassette is secured with two or more brackets across a structurally sound aluminum housing, providing a more reliable installation.

Recessed Pockets

The recessed pocket is a very popular top treatment among architects and contractors (if the space allows). Similar to the cassette, the shade roller, fabric, brackets, and power cords are hidden in the aluminum enclosure. The aluminum pocket comes in basic colors or can be custom colored. To access the shade, there is a removable closure plate.

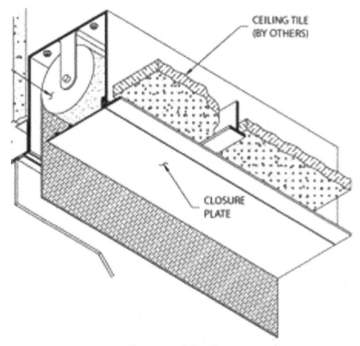

Recessed Pocket

Carpenters can also fabricate the pocket on site using sheetrock and plywood blocking with a stand-alone closure plate and bracket. While this is an option, the handmade pocket usually is never truly square and may cause mounting problems for the closure plate.

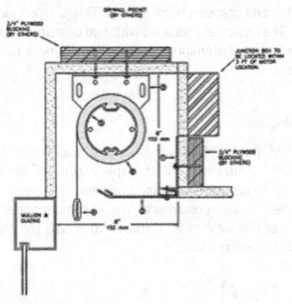

Site-Fabricated Pocket

Finishes

All of the aluminum top treatments—the open roll, cassettes and the recessed pocket—are available in popular standard colors (white, black, anodized aluminum, and ivory). Custom powder-coated colors are possible for any project.

Interior Louver Solutions

There is a long history of horizontal louver blinds, beginning with the venetian blind. There was a great revival in the seventies with the introduction of the one-inch mini blind in a rainbow of colors. While there is not much interest today from a decorative perspective, the horizontal louver for both interior and exterior is finding its place as engineered shading solutions (exterior louver solutions are discussed in the chapter "Exterior Shading Solutions").

Solutions with horizontal louvers offer advantages over roller shades. With wide blades of aluminum, solar heat gain can be reduced by more than 90 percent. The louvers have multiple benefits.

- Louvers bounce natural daylight deep into the space.
- Annoying glare is reduced.
- UV rays are blocked.
- Tilting the louvers offers both privacy and a view.
- Manual and motorized louvers are available.

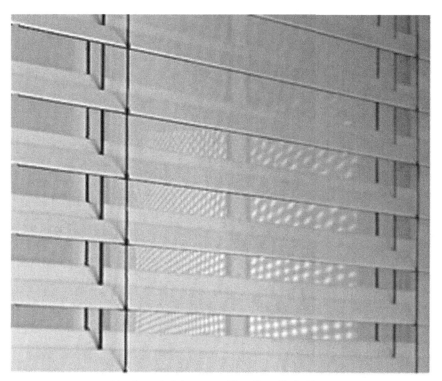

Horizontal Louver Shading Solution

Chapter 6

Skylight Shading Solutions

Skylight shading solutions are available in many shapes, sizes, and orientations. Skylight shading systems are challenged with orientations that need to function without the assistance of gravity. This is when tensioned solutions are required. Tensioned systems keep the fabric taut regardless of slope or angle with minimal sagging. These systems allow for great flexibility and cover a variety of conditions as shown below.

Skylight Shapes

A common tensioned system works with two rollers, one motor, sidetracks, and pulling straps. The tube with the motor does the pulling of the bottom shade bar; the other roller provides the tension with springs.

Tensioned Skylight System

Skylight shading solutions can be used as both solar or blackout. Blackout skylight solutions require wider sidetracks for the fabric to slip in to, preventing light seepage. The fabrics provide control over solar heat gain, light, and glare. Details about the fabrics are included in the chapter "Fabric Technologies."

As far as controls, these systems are available with manual crank control, but they work best with motorization. All types of automated controls are available from wireless technology to home-automation integration (see "Smart Controls").

The Tensioned Zip Skylight Shade

To understand what the tensioned Zip skylight shade is, let me first explain a Zip shade. The Zip shading solution is manufactured with a "zipper-like" detail welded to the vertical edges of the fabric. These zippers run in tracks on each side and prevent the fabric from falling out or being pushed out of the aluminum side channels.

In order to keep constant tension on the fabric, there must be a way to pull the fabric taut. On the double-roller system, this is done with a spring (as shown previously). The tensioned hembar eliminates the need for the fixed roller with the spring. Instead, the hembar provides the tension. This works well for many applications, especially as a skylight or a bottom-up shade. Once we add the Zip feature, we have an engineered shading solution that needs no fixed support bars to prevent sagging and only one roller for the shade rollup. The result is a clean, elegant, and reliable skylight system that can use with a mesh or blackout fabric.

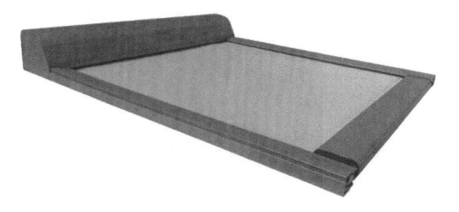

Zip Skylight

The tensioned Zip shade is an engineering breakthrough. Not only can it be used to cover skylights, this system also works well as a bottom-up shade. In addition to the various interior solutions, this product is also suitable for exterior installations.

Bottom-Up Shades

The bottom-up shading systems also employ the tensioned hembar solution. As described above, the tensioned Zip is an excellent product for shades traveling from the bottom of the window to the top. Another tensioned solutions works similarly, but it is not a Zip shade. This shade can work with cables or guide rails. However, there will be light gaps between the fabric and the rails (unlike the Zip shade).

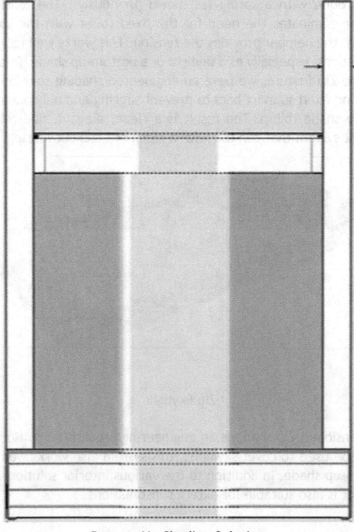

Bottom-Up Shading Solution

Trapezoid Blinds and Shades

There are few operable solutions for trapezoid-shaped windows. Presented here are two types: the rack arm system and the tensioned cable shade system. Both solutions can be installed on the interior or exterior.

The rack arm system is a nonretractable louver system. The louvers can open and close to control solar energy, light, and glare. It is very beneficial when precise light control is important in venues such as galleries or museums. Each system incorporates standard components but is custom designed to meet the specific application requirements.

This reliable solution offers years of dependable service with minimal required maintenance. It is perfect for difficult glazing problems—no matter the slope or angle of the window. The system can be used in just about any glazing situation—horizontal, inclined, vertical—and with any shape of window opening.

Rack Arm System

The tensioned cable shade system provides an adaptable compact solution. The shade works well for angled top windows because it functions well as a bottom-up shade. In fact, this shade works in any direction. The ultra-thin cables maintain the fabric tension and the ability for the fabric to follow the shape of the glazing.

Chapter 7

Blackout Shading Solutions

The main purpose for a blackout shading solution is to create a pitch-black space that allows no light seepage through the windows. This begins with an opaque fabric, which means that no light is able to pass through it. In the chapter "Fabric Technologies," details on the unique attributes of the blackout fabric will be presented.

Blackout with Seepage

The other challenge in creating total blackout is to address the gaps around a typical roller shade (see photo above). To eliminate the gaps, a shade cassette is specified for the space above the shade roller, and sidetracks are used for the gaps on the sides.

The sidetracks allow for the blackout fabric to be inserted inside. They are made with aluminum, come in the same finishes as the cassette, and are available in custom color finishes. The architectural details are shown below.

The best system for achieving a blackout condition is the Zip shade (described in the previous chapter). With the zipper-like design, the fabric is secured into the side channels and will not fall out. This can be installed as either an interior or exterior installation.

Chapter 8

Dual Shading Solutions

Dual Shading Solutions combine a solar shade and a blackout shade in the same opening, which provides a wide range of light control. Dual Shading Solutions are great for bedrooms, guest rooms, conference rooms, classrooms, and health care.

The typical configuration of a Dual Shading Solution is the blackout shade mounted over the solar shade (as shown below). Notice the slight offsetting, which allows the upper fabric to clear the bottom roller.

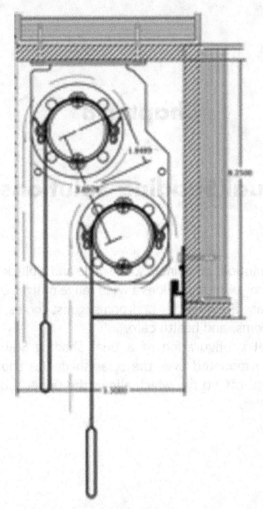

Typical Dual Shade Configuration

This works fine except when the ceiling condition does not allow for the eight inches of height required. Another option is the tandem arrangement (as seen below). The problem with this solution is that the solar shade fabric is very far from the glass, which leaves an awkward appearance.

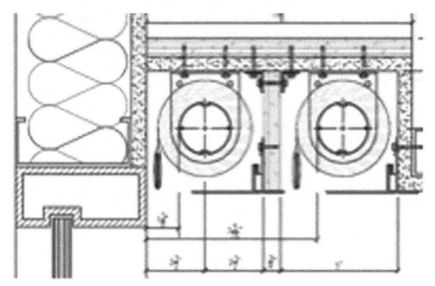

Tandem Dual Shade Configuration

A clever solution is to utilize a secondary roller that allows the blackout fabric to snake around the solar shade fabric so both cloths are now close to the glass. The drawing below shows this concept.

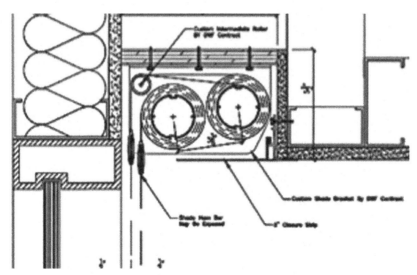

Dual Shade with Redirect Roller

The Dual Shading Solution is available with manual or automated controls. A wide range of solar shades and blackout fabrics are also available. Both controls and fabrics are explained in detail in subsequent chapters.

Chapter 9

Exterior Shading Solutions

Exterior shading solutions are in their infancy in the United States. Architects are now being introduced to the innovative European systems that provide superior performance for the reduction of solar heat gain. All across Europe (including northern climates), exterior shading solutions are seen on the most sustainable buildings.

Exterior Shading Solution

Exterior shading solutions are gaining popularity because of their superior performance in reducing solar heat gain. The graphic below tells it all. A space with no shades allows 80 percent solar heat gain, an interior shading solution allows more than 50 percent solar heat gain, and an exterior shading solution blocks between 80 and 90 percent.

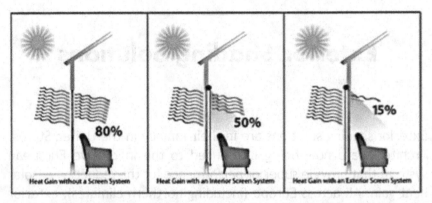

Heat Gain without a Screen System	Heat Gain with an Interior Screen System	Heat Gain with an Exterior Screen System

Solar Heat Gain Performance of an Exterior Shading Solution

The exterior shading hardware described for this chapter will describe the cable-guided system, which is a typical roller with hembar, a tensioned system, which works without the assistance of gravity and can be installed for any orientation and finally the Zip shade, an innovative system where the fabric is locked into the guide rails.

Cable-Guided Exterior Shading Solution

The cable-guided exterior shading solution is a motorized system with an elegantly designed tubular cassette, which adds an attractive architectural element to today's dynamic facades. The aluminum housing protects the roller shade components from the elements. The shade has a telescopic bottom bar that slides along the stainless steel side cables. The cassette and cable brackets are designed to integrate with the facade.

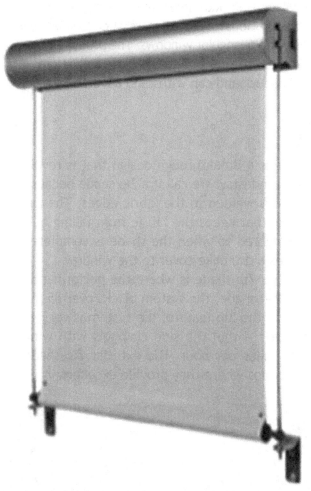

Cable-Guided Exterior Shade

The fabrics used for exterior shading solutions provide double resistance to warp and weft stretching and are not subject to any deformation. More about this fabric is included in the chapter "Fabric Technologies."

Exterior Tension System

The exterior shading solution tension system is an innovative shading system designed for horizontal, inclined, and vertical glazing. Its unique tensioning device keeps fabric flat and taut over wide and

51

long spans of glazing. Moreover, the system provides the ability to customize applications on curved glass (such as solariums), irregularly shaped glass, and triangular windows. The product is very reliable and can be used for both interior and exterior applications. It is a durable, heavy-duty product and can withstand adverse weather conditions.

Zip Shade

The Zip shade is a breakthrough design that is revolutionizing the window shade industry. We call it a Zip shade because a zipper-like locking device is welded to the fabric edges. The zipper slips into a side channel that keeps the fabric from falling out. The bottom hembar is weighted so when the shade is completely closed, the fabric provides a drumlike cover to the window.

The exterior Zip shade is where the performance soars. As an exterior window shade, the system blocks over 85 percent of solar heat gain. With the Zip feature, the system is very wind resistant. The fabric stays within the side channels with winds blowing at above eighty miles per hour. The exterior Zip shade also can be installed on patios where they provide excellent insect protection.

Tensioned Exterior Shading Solution

Exterior Louver Solutions

Exterior louver solutions have become one of the premier products in today's most sustainable buildings. The primary benefits of aluminum louvers, compared to roller shades, are the ability to tilt the louvers to provide harvesting of natural daylight into a space, the privacy achieved (along with a view) by tilting the louvers to prevent views into a space, and blocking nearly all of the solar heat gain with a highly reflective surface. These systems can be installed on the exterior of a building or within a double-glass facade.

A nice feature about the exterior louver blind with the robust extruded aluminum louvers is that it can span large widths without cords or ladders like a typical blind. The louvers are rotated and lifted by a tracking system concealed in the aluminum side channels. Within the channels is a patented chain-belt system that allows the louvers to be tilted into any position as well as raised or lowered.

Exterior Louver Solution

Rolling Aluminum Shutter

The rolling aluminum shutter is an elegant look at a previous clumsy solution. The ten-millimeter slats roll down narrow side channels. As they reach the bottom, the slats remain slightly apart, allowing light, air, and a view to the outside. As the slats close, the gaps seal up, blocking the light and securing the opening.

The rolling aluminum shutter operates like any exterior shading solution with a 120-volt motor put into action with a wired or wireless controller. The rolling aluminum shutter is available in standard or custom colors as well as ten-millimeter, twenty-five-millimeter, and fifty-millimeter slats.

Aluminum Rolling Shutter

Rack Arm

The rack arm system is a nonretractable louver system. The louvers can open and close to control solar energy, light, and glare. It is very beneficial when precise light control is important in venues such as galleries or museums. Each system incorporates standard components but is custom designed to meet the specific application requirements.

This reliable solution offers years of dependable service with minimal required maintenance. It is perfect for difficult glazing problems—no matter the slope or angle of the window. The system can be used in just about any glazing situation—horizontal, inclined, or vertical—and with any shape of window opening. The rack arm system can be used on interior or exterior windows.

Rack Arm Solution

Case Study

The gravity-assisted exterior shading solution was specified and installed at the 2010 Vancouver Winter Olympic Village. Below is my interview with the lead architect on that vast project.

Interview with Architect Roger Bayley

Vancouver, British Columbia, was the home of the 2010 Winter Olympics. The Olympic Athletes' Village, developed by Millennium Properties, is Canada's first truly sustainable community. The Olympic Village project is an example of how a contaminated industrial city center site can be transformed into a sustainable community.

The design manager for the project, Roger Bayley, worked with a team of five architectural firms to develop and implement the client's vision. Today, Roger leads his own firm in Vancouver and is dedicated to sustainable energy solutions. It was my pleasure to speak with Roger about his role with the Olympic project and what directed the team to specify and install exterior shading solutions.

NG: Why did you specify exterior shading solutions?

RB: It came from the concept of heating and cooling the residential units with German technology by using ceiling-mounted radiant heating and cooling. This technology requires hot and cold water to flow through capillary tubes above the ceiling drywall. In our modeling, we realized that at certain high levels of solar heat gain into the space, condensation could result on the drywall. The best way to reduce the solar heat gain and thereby eliminate the risk of condensation would be to install exterior solar shades. So, the exterior solar shades became part of the energy equation.

NG: Can you explain the concept of the radiant heating and cooling system?

RB: Radiant energy transfers heat from a mass with higher temperature to one with lower temperature, in the same way we are warmed by the sun. When the radiant system is switched to cooling, it draws heat from objects—including bodies—that are warmer, producing a cooling effect.

NG: How did installing the exterior shading solutions contribute to achieving the LEED Gold designation?

RB: It was a part of the overall design that included the radiant ceilings, which enabled the project to earn points for energy efficiency and innovation in design. The entire project received LEED Platinum certification, and the buildings earned LEED Gold status.

NG: What performance capabilities did you require from the exterior shading solutions?

RB: The project was complex. We needed a solution that could perform under adverse weather conditions, provide the energy reduction required, enhance the building's exterior design, and stand up to the test of time. The shades are controlled automatically with a combination of sun and wind sensors. The components, which include side cables, can withstand severe wind gusts, and the fabric provides the solar protection needed. The design elements, such as the enclosure and wall brackets, enhance the building facade.

NG: How do you see the future of sustainable building incorporating engineered shading solutions?

RB: To begin with, shades cannot be an afterthought. They must be planned for from the beginning of the design stage. The key to an engineered shading solution is automation and integration into building systems. The shades need to be incorporated into the energy efficiency of the building. This requires good statistical data to prove the performance of the shading solutions. This is challenging to achieve at the outset of the design process.

Case Study

The gravity-assist shades were installed at Aufgang Architects new building in Suffern, New York. Below is my interview with Ariel Aufgang, principal of Aufgang Architects.

Interview with Ariel Aufgang of Aufgang Architects

I grew up and still live and work in Rockland County, a northwestern suburb of New York City. So, when Ariel Aufgang called me to inquire about our exterior shading solutions, I was excited since his architecture firm is located just a few minutes away. Below is my interview with Ariel, the principal of Aufgang Architects.

NG: What is the background of Aufgang Architects?

AA: The firm was founded in 1971. I started as an intern in 1997, working winters and summers for five years. When I graduated from college in 2001, I started working full-time, I became a partner in 2009, and I bought the firm in 2012. Today, we have twenty-four full-time architects in our office.

NG: Describe the type of projects you specialize in?

AA: Aufgang Architects focuses on mixed-use, commercial, and multifamily projects. Many of our projects are in New York City, such as a mixed-use building on West Thirty-Fifth Street in Manhattan. With a total of 312 new units, commercial space, and parking, the project should add much-needed housing and services to this fast-growing neighborhood.

NG: How does sustainable design enter into your projects?

AA: Sustainable design is one of our guiding principles. We look at sustainable design initially from the most basic aspects of building with an initial focus on efficient HVAC systems, effective insulation, which includes the number one area of heat loss—the roof. Then, if the project calls for more sustainable systems, we may consider such things as geothermal heating, photovoltaic systems, and now exterior shading solutions. We designed and built New York City's first LEED Platinum affordable housing project, which employed solar panels and cogeneration energy strategies that utilize inexpensive fuels like natural gas to generate electricity in order to light and power the common areas and the waste heat from the generator to heat water for the building. So, that's one fuel source with two uses. The building also is designed to promote an *active design standard*. This is where we encourage the residents to do such things as using the stairs more and the elevator less; elevators are a large user of electricity in an apartment building. We installed glass doors at the staircase and added music and art to the stairwell to encourage this healthy alternative, and it's working!

NG: Tell me about your new building and what you are doing to promote sustainability?

AA: We are very excited with our new building, which is just now under construction. It's a chance for us to demonstrate the best sustainable ideas we have. The building will be super insulated with a geothermal system to provide a source for heat exchange with our ceiling-mounted heat pumps. This will eliminate the need for rooftop equipment, leaving us space for possible solar panels in the future.

NG: Why did you decide to add exterior shading solutions to your southern facade?

AA: Our new corporate headquarters will be located in downtown Suffern, New York. Not too long ago, I was buying something in a store not far from our building site. It was a bright, sunny day, and the store clerk was struggling with an annoying glare on the screen at the checkout. I began to pay attention to the other businesses along the street and saw an assortment of homemade solar force fields, which included poster board and tinfoil stuck to windows. I immediately thought, *This is the exact same southern exposure our building faces, and we can't struggle with glare and intense solar heat gain in a building that we have put so much emphasis on with sustainable ideas.* That is why I decided we needed some way to reduce the glare and provide sun protection to the southern facade. It makes no sense to invest into a state-of-the-art cooling system without some way to reduce the solar heat gain through the windows.

When I saw your exterior shading systems in a publication, I thought they would provide the protection needed by stopping the heat before it penetrated the glass—and also be a light touch to the design of the facade. Our brick envelope will have black window mullions, and your shades will be finished with a black aluminum cassette and black solar shade fabric, which will provide effective reduction in solar heat gain and glare as well as providing good visibility. I am also excited about the sun sensor, which will send a signal to the shades to lower based on the sun's intensity.

Chapter 10

The Zip Shade

The Zip shade is a breakthrough design that is revolutionizing the window shade industry. We call it a Zip shade because a zipper-like locking device is welded to the fabric edges. The zipper slips into a side channel that keeps the fabric from falling out. Since the bottom hembar is weighted, when the shade is completely closed, the fabric provides a drumlike cover to the window.

Zip Shade

With the fabric locked in, the Zip shade offers multiple advantages. A typical problem with a standard blackout shade with side channels is that the fabric never stays in the channel. A simple push on the fabric, and the cloth pops out, leaving a wrinkled condition. The blackout Zip never allows for this to occur, which is great for bedrooms, hotel rooms, or conference rooms.

The exterior Zip shade is where the performance soars. As an exterior window shade, the system blocks over 85 percent of solar heat gain. With the Zip feature, the system is very wind resistant. The fabric stays within the side channels with winds blowing at over eighty miles per hour. The exterior Zip shade also can be installed on patios to provide excellent insect protection.

To cover skylights the Skylight Shade is an industry breakthrough. With the locked-in fabric, the skylight shade needs no intermediate support bars to prevent sagging. The fabric remains taut even with large openings. The skylight Zip shade can be used with either mesh or blackout fabrics.

Finally there is the bottom-up shade. This is an interior shade that stacks at the bottom of the window and is pulled up to the top, allowing the window to be partially covered at the bottom, leaving the upper portion of the window open, a nice feature for privacy with a view.

Zip Insect Shade

Chapter 11

Shading for the Landscape Architect

There are many beautiful and creative ways landscape architects can provide natural shading solutions for their projects. However, when it comes to engineered solutions, such as those that are commonly used in pergolas, or where unusual shading structures require more creative approaches, the choices become somewhat limited. This article will explore a variety of new and exciting products from the resources of InSync Solar, experts in exterior solar shades.

The idea of an exterior shading solution is not a new one. A great example from history is a two thousand-year-old system found at the Roman Colosseum. If you have been fortunate enough to take a tour of this architectural wonder, you would have learned about the velarium. The velarium was a retractable fabric awning system to shade the spectators from the hot Italian sun.

The products presented here all are focused on providing shading for outdoor living environments. Many of these systems are often specified as a sustainable solution to reduce solar heat gain entering an interior living space as well.

Northwest of Venice is the city of Trento. It is the capital of Trentino and is located in the Adige River Valley. This historic city is the site of the MUSE Museum of Science complex, which the world-renowned architect Renzo Piano designed.

Throughout this large complex, more than six thousand exterior shades have been installed. The Renzo Piano Building Workshop designs many of their projects using such coverings. They also commonly customize basic functions of the products they specify. This includes the exterior shading solutions for the outdoor living spaces. For example, on the decks on the condos, they designed hockey-stick-shaped swing arms to project the gravity-assist exterior solar shades over the railing's edge. This clever alteration provided excellent shading along with good ventilation and unobstructed deck space.

Another interesting application for an exterior shading solution is installed on the patios. In the photo below, the Renzo Piano team wanted to provide a retractable shading system with cables. The tension-force system proved to be an excellent solution. Since a simple gravity-assist shade would sag as it rolled down, a device to provide tension to the fabric was required. The result was a taut, sloping shading system designed to mirror the surrounding Dolomite Mountains.

The Mar Adentro Hotel in Los Cabos, Mexico, is due to open this December. Designed by the architect Miguel Angel Aragones, this unique tourist destination features an eighty-three-suite, five-star hotel, as well as 106 private residences and eighteen estates. This one-of-a-kind architectural project is located in San Jose del Cabo, an enclave formed by desert and sea.

The complex is spread across a series of reflecting and infinity pools, the likes of which have not been seen anywhere. Also unique to the design is the wide use of exterior shading solutions throughout the project. Outdoor living and dining are the top reasons tourists visit tropical destinations. The cable-guided exterior shading solutions are installed to provide comfortable environments for lounging, socializing, and relaxing.

For public projects, outdoor common areas may require retractable shading devices. Another Renzo Piano Building Workshop example is at the Auditorium Parco della Musica in Rome. The exterior walkways are shaded with the tension-force skylight solution as shown below.

Tensioned Shading Solution

Today's pergolas are taking outdoor living to levels of luxury comparable to the Caesars of Rome. Systems with rotating louvers, drainage systems for rain, built-in LED lights, and heaters are available. Below are a few systems showing louvers and retractable canopy systems.

Interview with Jennifer Birkeland of West 8 Landscape Architects

Exterior shading solutions are a significant consideration for landscape architects. In order to learn more about this specialized discipline, I interviewed Jennifer Birkeland of West 8. West 8 is an award-winning international office for urban design and landscape architecture, which was founded in 1987. Over the last twenty-eight years, West 8 has established itself as a leading practice with an international team of seventy architects, urban designers, landscape architects, and industrial engineers. West 8 has developed projects all over the world, including Copenhagen, London, Moscow, New York, Madrid, Toronto, and Amsterdam.

NG: Who is West 8, and what is your role?

JB: West 8 is an international, award-winning multidisciplinary design firm with offices in Rotterdam, New York, and Brussels. I am currently a project manager in the New York office.

NG: What are some of West 8's most recognized projects?

JB: West 8 has a wide range of projects completed around the world. Each project has its own approach and identity. Some of our award-winning projects include the redevelopment of Toronto's Central Waterfront, New York's Governors Island, Madrid RIO, Schouwburgplein in Rotterdam, and Miami Beach's Soundscape Park.

NG: How does West 8 incorporate engineered shading solutions into its designs?

LB: Providing shade is often a crucial requirement in landscape architecture. From plants to engineered solutions, we often critically analyze the site restraints and the program requirements to identify where including shade is most appropriate for the design.

NG: Are there any projects in the planning stages that will incorporate exterior shading solutions?

JB: Currently we are working on the design for the future Houston Botanical Gardens. It is a multiacre project embedded with specific requirements and an extensive landscape and building program. The spaces require a high level of flexibility, and shade is necessary in such a subtropical climate.

Chapter 12

Shading for the passive house

After years of popularity throughout Europe, the passive house is finally hitting the shores of the USA. We are seeing new projects being designed and built by architects and contractors who are trained specifically for this exciting technology. In fact, the tallest passive house in the world is being built in New York City on Roosevelt Island for the new Cornell Tech housing facility.

A primary goal of a passive house is to reduce the energy costs of the building by 90 percent. Designers of the passive house are using a variety of tools to achieve this goal. One of these tools includes exterior shading solutions and specifically exterior solar shades.

One of the biggest challenges for a passive-house design is the glazing and solar heat gain passing through. While this works well in the winter months where you want that low sun to radiate heat into the space, the solar radiation needs to be blocked on east and west windows during summer months with exterior shading solutions.

Of course, the high summer sun also is effectively controlled by exterior shading that blocks up to 90 percent of all solar heat gain when used with the properly selected shade fabrics. Using mesh fabrics allows the preservation of the exterior views and can allow outside ventilation air to easily pass through to interior spaces.

A particular effective solution is the exterior Zip shade, which can perform double duty as an exterior shade and an insect screen. The Zip shade is a breakthrough design that is revolutionizing the window-shade industry. We call it a Zip shade because a zipper-like locking device is welded to the fabric edges. The zipper slips into a side channel that keeps the fabric from falling out. The bottom hembar is weighted so when the shade is completely closed, the fabric provides a drumlike cover to the window.

With the fabric locked in, the Zip shade offers multiple advantages. A typical problem with a standard blackout shade with side channels is that the fabric never stays in the channel. A simple push on the fabric, and the cloth pops out, leaving a wrinkled condition. The Zip blackout shade never allows for this to occur, which is great for bedrooms, hotel rooms, conference rooms, and classrooms.

The exterior Zip shade is where the performance soars. As an exterior window shade, the system blocks more than 90 percent of solar heat gain. With the Zip feature, the system is very wind resistant. The fabric stays within the side channels with winds blowing at over eighty miles per hour. The InSync ZIP Exterior Shade with a mesh fabric also can be installed on patios and provides excellent insect protection.

Extreme wind tunnel testing confirms the retention ability of the Zip system and attachment components. While we would never recommend leaving exterior shades deployed in such conditions, it is comforting to know the durability and performance engineered into the system. Where the system is placed close to the faced glass, the deformation of the fabric is even less noticeable since both the shade fabric and the structural glazing share the wind force.

To cover overhead skylights, the skylight shade is an industry breakthrough. With the locked-in fabric, the skylight shade needs no intermediate support bars to prevent sagging. The fabric remains taut even with large openings. The skylight Zip shade can be used with either mesh or blackout fabrics.

Finally, there is the bottom-up shade. This is an interior shade the stacks at the bottom of the window and is pulled up to the top, allowing the window to be partially covered at the bottom and leaving the upper portion of the window open. This is a nice feature for privacy with a view.

Interview with Lois Arena of Steven Winter Associates

I recently had the pleasure of sitting down with Lois Arena, the senior mechanical engineer for Steven Winter Associates. She is one of the leading passive-house consultants in the country. Lois is the passive-house consultant on the world's tallest and largest passive house for Cornell's new technical campus on Roosevelt Island.

NG: How did you get involved in this exciting new field of passive house?

LA: My undergraduate degree was from the University of Connecticut in resource management. I received my master's in mechanical engineering from the University of Colorado with a focus on energy use in buildings. My first job was with the state energy office for six years, and then I got my general contractor's license and did some remodeling jobs on spec for eight or nine years. Then I contacted Steven Winter right after the market crash, and that's when I started working here. My engineering background was perfect.

My work here evolved from research to passive-house consulting. It started about five years ago when we received some inquiries from clients about passive house. This motivated me to get certified, and as soon as I did, we received a request to consult on a passive-house project in Ithaca, New York. It was for seven homes and was a great learning experience for us. It snowballed from there, with us getting the Cornell project, which will be the tallest and largest passive house in the world.

NG: Where do you see the fastest growth in passive house?

LA: The exposure from Cornell has given us great exposure. But the biggest area of growth has been in the affordable-housing market. I have to give credit to Tim McDonald from Pennsylvania. He is with a major university in the state, and he has been working with the Pennsylvania Housing Authority to get passive house as a tax credit option on the project team's application. This has spurred a lot of work for us all throughout the state. Eight of the thirty-two affordable homes that were approved will be passive house. Tim has been reaching out to surrounding states to get the same type of passive-house tax-credit options.

NG: What are your thoughts about the New York City mayor's plan for "One City: Built to Last"?

LA: New York City has established very aggressive carbon goals. In order to meet these goals, there will need to be very extreme actions, and this will take time. This past April, we went to Brussels to see how they are achieving similar carbon goals. Brussels has adopted passive house as their building code. They started this process ten years ago, and today, all new construction in Brussels must be passive house.

NG: How important are exterior shading solutions for the passive house?

LA: When we were in Brussels, the exterior shades were everywhere, basically a building standard. For the passive house in general, exterior shades help balance out the solar heat gain conditions from winter to summer. We want the solar heat in the wintertime. In fact, the windows for passive house are designed to allow the solar heat gain to enter through the glass during the winter. Obviously that needs to be controlled in the summer months, and exterior shades work best for those conditions.

Chapter 13

Fabric Technologies

A great deal of the success of engineered shading solutions rests with the choice of the fabrics. In this chapter, reference will be given to fabrics that control solar heat gain, light, and glare and are manufactured without the environmentally damaging plastic PVC.

Controlling Solar Heat Gain

Solar shade fabric is a good place to start with the challenge of controlling solar heat gain into a room. In winter, we want the shades raised to allow the solar radiation to heat up the cold spaces. In warmer months, the solar heat gain needs to be controlled.

Solar shade fabric fights solar heat gain on several fronts: openness of weave, color of the fabric, and innovative reflective material. Let's start with openness. Solar shade fabrics are manufactured with a variety of openness, such as 3, 5, and 10 percent open. A 5 percent openness means that 95 percent of the cloth is closed. As you can imagine, the tighter the weave, the more solar heat gain protection the fabric provides.

In choosing openness, the decision is influenced by the orientation of the windows. Northern-facing windows need the least protection (10 percent openness is suitable). For exposures with direct sunlight, 3 or 5 percent is required to effectively reduce solar heat gain.

Visual Transmittance

Selecting an openness alone based on orientation may lead to disappointment. The color of the fabric plays a role in the amount of light entering a room. This is called *visual transmittance*. To compare, take the same fabric with the same openness (one in white and one in black). The white color brightens the room more than the black because the darker colors absorb more of the light. Therefore, choosing a fabric based on openness alone may not provide the desired solution.

The color can significantly affect the performance of a fabric in reducing solar heat gain. As we all know, lighter colors reflect light and darker colors absorb light, which converts into solar heat gain. A white color 5 percent open fabric allows 49 percent solar heat gain with a one-inch clear glass window. Comparing this with a black fabric shows 56 percent solar heat gain. Clearly, the lighter the color the fabric, the better solar heat gain reduction.

Glare Control

Glare is caused by a significant ratio of luminance between the visual task and the glare source. A solar shade will reduce the disparity in light levels, such as in between a computer screen and a window. To understand the cause of glare, let's take a look at the 1:3:10 Luminance Ratio Rule, which states that the ratio of light levels between the visual task and an adjacent surface needs to be less than 1:3, and that the light level between a visual task and a nonadjacent surface should fall within a 1:10 ratio.

In the photo below, the room without an interior shading solution, the light levels fall way beyond the 1:3:10 Luminance Ratio Rule, and the result is glare. However, with glare-reducing fabrics, the levels are corrected, which reduces the glare by as much as 95 percent.

Let's compare the same fabric in the same colors as our previous example on solar heat gain control. A white 5 percent open fabric will reduce glare by 57 percent, and a black fabric reduces glare by 90 percent. Clearly, the darker color has a significant advantage in reducing glare over light colors because the darker color absorbs the light.

Metalized Fabrics

An innovative, highly effective solution that reduces solar heat gain and glare regardless of interior color is metalized fabric. The technique is to apply a highly reflective, ultra-fine layer of aluminum onto the screen fabric to dramatically improve the solar energy performance. A light color reduces glare by 82 percent and solar heat gain by 45 percent. The dark color reduces glare by 95 percent and solar heat gain by 42 percent.

A new technology offers the same attributes and results with a metalized thread woven into the cloth construction, eliminating the process of applying the aluminum layer to the fabric.

Transparency

One of the benefits of solar shade fabrics is the transparency or the ability to see through the fabric itself. Of course, this transparency is regulated by the openness, but it is also determined by the color. In the picture below, the top row is white fabric in a series of openness of 1, 3, 5, and 10 percent. The bottom row is the same arrangement of openness. Clearly the black fabric provides better transparency than the white color.

Transparency comparison of white versus black fabric

The ability to see through the fabric is an advantage of solar shade fabrics. It is important to remember that there is a trade-off between seeing through the fabric with a larger openness in exchange for allowing too much solar heat gain.

Blackout Fabrics

As the name implies, blackout fabric allows no light to pass through the material, and it comes in various colors besides black. The process of manufacturing blackout was invented by Baltimore-based Rockland Industries and involves coating a fabric with layers of foam (passes). A two-pass blackout is produced by applying two passes of foam to a fabric. First, a black layer is applied to the fabric, and then a white or light-colored layer is applied on top of the black. A three-pass blackout is produced by applying a layer of white foam to the fabric first and then a layer of black foam, followed by the third and final layer of white or light-colored foam. A common misconception is that blackout fabric is black in color. Actually, the process allows many colors to be produced.

PVC-Free Fabrics

Why should we avoid fabrics with PVC? According to Greenpeace,

> This commonplace plastic is one of the biggest contributors to the flood of toxic substances saturating our planet and its inhabitants. PVC contaminates humans and the environment throughout its lifecycle during its production, use, and disposal. While all plastics pose serious threats to human health and the environment, few realize that PVC is the single most environmentally damaging of all plastics. Since safer alternatives are available for virtually all uses of PVC, it is possible to protect human health and the environment by replacing and eventually phasing out this poison plastic.
> Source: http://www.greenpeace.org/usa/Global/usa/report/2009/4/pvc-the-poison-plastic.html

The history of PVC in the window-covering industry is seen in shade cloth, drapery fabric, and vertical blinds. Eco-conscious manufacturers offer alternatives to this deadly material. Today, there is a wide selection of PVC-free fabrics for all types of engineered shading solutions that control solar heat gain, glare, and light.

Recycled Fabrics

GreenScreen Revive is a revolutionary new sustainable window shade fabric. GreenScreen Revive combines sustainable values with outstanding performance and has been Cradle-to-Cradle Certified. This certification is a term coined by McDonough Braungart Design Chemistry, which describes the product's life cycle from creation to recreation. GreenScreen Revive offers excellent solar control, reduces heat and glare, and offers a remarkably clean view through to the outdoors owing to its finely knitted weaves.

This fire-retardant, PVC-free fabric is constructed of 100 percent polyester yarn, with a minimum of 89 percent Repreve polyester. Repreve is recycled and recyclable, contains low VOCs, and is made in the USA. Twelve sixteen-ounce water bottles produce enough yarn to weave one yard of fabric.

Flame-Retardant Fabrics

Fabrics used in most public spaces, including schools, churches, auditoriums, and theaters, are required by law in many states and cities to be certified as flame retardant, according to standards developed by the National Fire Protection Association (NFPA). NFPA has various standards depending on how the fabric will be used. In the case of draperies, curtains, and similar hanging textiles, the standard that applies is NFPA 701: Standard Methods of Fire Tests for Flame Propagation of Textiles and Films. This test measures the flammability of a fabric when it is exposed to specific sources of ignition.

Exterior Fabrics

Exterior shading solutions require fabrics that can withstand the elements and perform under constant tension. The best fabrics for exterior shading solution are from Serge Ferrari. Their fabric uses a technology they call Precontraint. It is a high-tenacity polyester micro-yarn base cloth coating of the warp and weft threads under a high-performance polymer surface layer. This technique provides exceptional dimensional stability, long-term strength, and exceptional flatness. The Serge Ferrari fabrics can be seen on the London Olympic Stadium roof as well as many other prestigious projects worldwide.

Exterior Shade Fabric

Interview with Brian Foley of Serge Ferrari Fabrics

Serge Ferrari is the worldwide leader in exterior fabrics. To learn more, I had the pleasure of interviewing Brian Foley, the regional manager of the northeast United States. Brian has been with Serge Ferrari for nine years.

NG: Can you tell me about Serge Ferrari, its history, and what markets it serves?

BF: Ferrari Textiles was founded by Serge Ferrari in 1974. Ferrari Textiles was rebranded as Serge Ferrari in 2012. Its cooperate headquarters and manufacturing facilities are located in La Tour du Pin, France. There are two additional manufacturing facilities in Switzerland. Serge Ferrari's recycling facility, Texyloop, is in Italy as well as fourteen additional offices and stocking warehouses throughout the world, including Pompano Beach, Florida.

Serge Ferrari is a leader in the "flexible composite material" sector. Their corporate mission is to ensure a global offering to meet tomorrow's major challenges, such as sustainable construction, energy control, protection, and renewal of resources.

Serge Ferrari is a vertically integrated company mastering all the production steps from product development to recycling, raw material formulation, process and mechanical engineering, spinning, formulation, coating and extrusion, logistics, and recycling of end-of-life products.

The company offers solutions to the demands for countless markets with products designed for acoustic solutions, composite building skins, solar protection, bio-climatic facade, breathable membranes, modular structures, visual communication, indoor and outdoor furniture, yachting protection, environmental protection, and specialty membranes.

NG: The Precontraint process is an exclusive offering of Serge Ferrari. Can you tell me why this is a superior fabric for exterior shading solutions?

BF: Precontraint is patented technology developed by Serge Ferrari. We offer a number of different products utilizing Precontraint technology. Precontraint allows Serge Ferrari to apply equal tension across the WARP (length) and WEFT (width) throughout the entire coating process giving our products superior dimensional stability.

In terms of shading solutions, Precontraint provides a number of unique advantages for a number of different applications. With regard to the commercial awning and the pergola markets, Precontraint products are an obvious choice due to their ability to protect against UV degradation and abrasion. Precontraint also allows the fabric to lay flat, allowing better welds. The reason most often given for why to use a Precontraint product is the dimensional stability.

Interior and exterior shade applications will also benefit from using Precontraint. Soltis, one of the many Precontraint products, is designed specifically for these applications. The fact that Precontraint fabrics are woven first and then coated creates thinner and lighter options, which allows more fabric into a smaller cassette, which will potentially reduce the size of the motor. The dimensional stability prevents edge curling and will not require resetting of limit switches.

NG: How do you see the growth of the exterior shading solutions in the US market?

BF: There is tremendous growth in the exterior shade market in the United States. As people and companies look to reduce energy costs, this market is starting to become an obvious win. Serge Ferrari products are excellent at reducing solar heat gain and glare while also providing an aesthetic benefit due to the wide choice of fabric color options.

Chapter 14

Smart Controls

Vast improvements in motor-control technology have allowed motorized window coverings to become mainstream. Owners and architects are often confronted with a confusing array of equipment and solution choices. Engineering a system within the constraints of a budget usually requires the assistance of a shading consultant who can balance functionality, cost, and overall performance. When executed correctly, an intelligent shading control system increases occupant comfort while saving money on summer cooling, winter heating, and year-round lighting.

Motorized Window Coverings

Motorized window coverings have become a standard for much of the architectural community. Once only found in high-end commercial and residential properties, they are now routinely specified for a wide array of projects and budgets.

This shift is mostly the by-product of lightweight construction and the trend toward larger windows. Structures completely clad in glass and the demands for spectacular views with floor-to-ceiling windows are becoming the norm. The resulting structures are often stunning examples of how great architectural design can transform how buildings are viewed and how we interact with them.

The use of a glass facade presents a unique challenge for architects. How do you control the immense energy generated by lots of glass and full sunlight? The glare and heat generated by the sun can quickly turn a great-looking building or space into a hellish nightmare. We need to accept that window coverings are no longer just decorative but a complete building system on par with lighting and HVAC.

Random Shade Strategy vs. Engineered Shading

The Motorization Continuum

Motorization of window coverings may seem like a simple task, however, owners, architects, and electricians often have a poor understanding of the process. The term *motorization* is often used to describe all sorts of solution sets, and the gap between expectation and outcome often becomes an expensive point of contention.

In reality, motorization is a continuum with transitions from basic motorization to automation and ultimately to integration. It represents the incremental application of "intelligent" hardware and software needed to control the system in a more complicated manner. There is usually a lack of understanding of the complexity and cost to engineer a properly functioning system. The additional layers of control do not add cost in a linear manner, and seemingly small changes in functionality can add significantly to the overall budget.

Basic Motorization

At the core of motorization is replacing manual controls with a motor. Shade motors are inherently "dumb" devices that respond to applications of voltage to send the shade up or down. A switch that applies and reverses the flow of electricity as needed controls the motor.

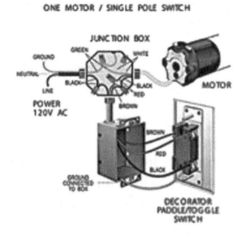

ONE MOTOR / SINGLE POLE SWITCH

For many applications, basic motorization is a perfectly valid solution and requires minimal engineering. Most shade motors have internal limit switches that stop movement at manually set points. This is the only concession to "intelligence" provided for at this level of motor control.

The basic 120-volt system is controlled in one of two ways:

1. *Supervised switching*—using a three-position momentary contact wall switch. This provides positive user control and is the preferred control method with larger shades in public spaces. Supervised switching has become important with the advent of litigation initiated by children becoming entangled in window treatments. Many shade motors have enough torque to injure small children. Releasing the switch immediately stops motor movement and provides an enhanced level of safety.

2. *Unsupervised switching*—using a maintained contact three-position switch. This is best described as "set and forget" where the shades move on their own to the preset limit settings. This is an acceptable switching method in a private building where there is more certainty about who will be near the moving shade cloth. Remember that sudden shade movement can often startle building occupants. It is best to use on shades ninety-six inches or more above the finished floor line or in buildings where occupants know how the shades will operate.

Low-Voltage Motors

Low-voltage motors requiring twenty-four volts also fall into basic motorization. The main difference is that they operate on a constant connection to 24 volts DC with the switching done by a simple logic circuit located in the motor. These motors often have the ability to stop at a programmed intermediate position.

Battery-Powered Motors

Battery-powered motors are usually 12-volt DC devices that can be utilized in locations where hard wiring is all but impossible. A lithium-ion battery can power these types of motors for up to five years with the use of two or three cycles per day. The only limitation is they are reserved for smaller shades in locations where the batteries can easily be accessed. Some systems have even adapted the use of solar cells to continuously recharge the batteries and minimize maintenance.

Coupled Roller Shades in Basic Motorization

When possible, the 120-volt motors have enough power to move many shades coupled together. This reduces the number of motors and switches needed to control large window areas. It also eliminates lots of additional wiring and outlets.

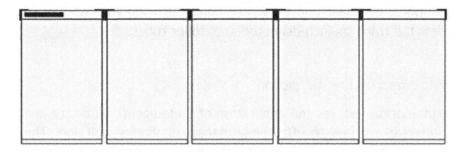

Coupled roller shades should be used where individual control is not an issue and where the owner likes to have uniform shade appearance. The limit on the number of shades that can be coupled together is usually five, but it can be fewer based on size and overall weight of the combined shade cloth.

Shade Motor Facts for Basic Motorization

When engineering and specifying basic motorization, we need to remember that motors come in all shapes, sizes, and ratings. Shade motors in a range of lifting capacities are measured in newton meters (Nm). A newton meter is equal to .737 foot-pounds or 8.85 inch-pounds and is used in calculating the area and/or weight of shade cloth that can be lifted by a particular motor.

Low-voltage motors have lower Nm ratings and usually cannot be coupled together. The standard 24-volt motor is usually rated at 2 Nm, but gearing down the motor speed can increase that number.

Limit Switch   Capacitance   Brake   Motor   Gearbox

The 120-volt motors are designed to be more robust with capacitor start motors and a series of reduction gears that provide lift up to 100 Nm and more depending on manufacturer. These motors routinely lift shades up to twenty-eight feet wide and twenty-two feet tall using six-inch-diameter steel roller tubes.

Motorized Shade Automation

Automation involves the application of "intelligent" hardware and software overlays to effectively manage a shading solution. The concept is to reduce the amount of human input required to make multiple devices work as one in a variety of ways.

At the very bottom of the automation process is having multiple shades operate off of one wall switch. It is always amazing to see a room full of window shades operate in lockstep unison by simply flipping a switch. ISO relays are required in order to protect the motors from the destructive electrical feedback caused by collapsing magnetic fields generated when their limit switches suddenly turn off the motors.

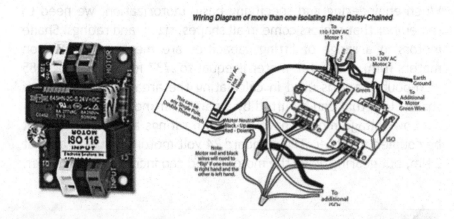

ISO relays can be panelized to control multiples of four shade motors at a time and are a convenient way of placing controls in a central location for easy diagnostics and repairs. They may also be located at each motor power drop to minimize wiring runs and "value engineer" the system layout.

Low-voltage motors can be easily controlled without ISO relays because of the basic motor control built into them. Rather than controlling multiple motors by switching power on and off, the signal control lines for the individual motors are simply wired into one switch. As the diagram below indicates, many different types of window coverings can take advantage of low-voltage motors without the use of additional control equipment.

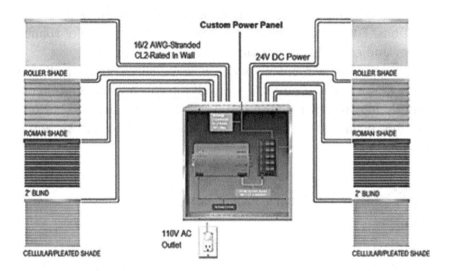

Automation by Intelligent Motor Grouping

The basic control groups fall into three categories:

1. *Local Control.* Each shade can be controlled individually, or within the context of small-localized groups, by one switch (for example, all the shades in a particular office or room).

2. *Group Control.* Multiple shades in multiple areas can be programmed to respond together from one switch (for example, all the shades on the south side of the building). This can also be extended to a group consisting of all the windows on floor seven.

3. *Master Control.* All of the shades in the project programmed to respond to one switch (for example, raising all the shades for window cleaning or lowering them for security at the end of the workday).

Wireless Intelligent Control

Wireless devices have dramatically changed our world, and the list of wireless devices grows each year. The window-covering industry has also benefited from this revolution with a variety of unique solutions. For many projects, the expense and difficulty of running power and control wiring is simply out of the question.

Advances in microprocessor design and engineering have allowed shade motor manufacturers to place all the control and radio circuits directly into the motor. The result is a powerful system that only requires power to the motors; the rest of the control system is wireless.

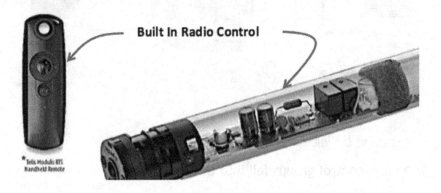

Built In Radio Control

*Telis Modulis RTS
Handheld Remote

Many types of window coverings have motors adapted to this technology, and the motors are available in 120-, 24-, and 12-volt versions. Low-voltage motors are especially well suited for projects because electrical code regulations are similar to phone and network cable installations. Battery-powered systems work on twelve volts, making them completely autonomous and truly a wire-free solution.

The grouping functions allow up to sixteen different groups of motors, and each can be programmed for up to twelve different controllers. This flexibility offers clients an almost limitless combination of control based on their preferences.

There are many types of wall and tabletop controls available to meet client needs. Along with the handheld remotes, modern wireless systems fit nicely into any home office or small business setting. There is no need to worry about security because there are 16.7 million rolling codes used by the controllers to minimize unauthorized operation.

Smart-Device Control

The latest trend in window-covering control is the use of smart devices to directly control shading systems. Innovations such as Z Wave, ZigBee, Bluetooth, Wi-Fi Direct, and Mesh Network are the newest buzzwords in the industry. Each of these technologies promises to be the next biggest thing in shade control and ultimately home automation.

Higher-Level Automation

Up until now, our focus has been on basic-level automation with up-down-stop functionality for individual shades and larger groups. While this is a form of automation, it still places the decision-making process on the user. Higher levels of automation rely on intelligent devices to automatically make decisions within predefined parameters.

The ability to have timed events is an attractive addition to the automation continuum. Almost all projects would benefit from the ability to have shades deploy and retract at preset times of the day. When used correctly, timers can contribute greatly to energy-conservation schemes and provide consistent, measurable savings.

The advent of LEED has made the use of timers mandatory to get points for energy reduction, light management, and light-pollution reduction. When timed events are consistently used across the breadth of the project, they can add significant LEED points to the project scoreboard.

Sun sensors are also an attractive add-on to the automation scheme. The augmentation of building automation with these devices takes maximum advantage of the sun's energy by allowing the maximum use of natural daylighting on cloudy days. Conversely, shade movement that is coordinated with the tracking of the sun across the sky can maximize the use of solar heating in the winter and mitigate the use of air conditioning during the summer.

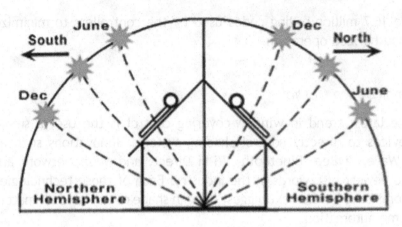

Building Automation and Control

Huge inroads have been made in the configuration and control of complete building systems. In the past, enormous HVAC systems were thrown into poorly designed buildings to manage occupant comfort, at least in theory. We have all experienced buildings with air conditioning so poorly designed and distributed that opening windows was the only way to control unmanageable systems.

Absolutely no consideration was given to designing buildings as an integrated system where the HVAC, lighting, and window coverings worked together in a carefully choreographed manner. Until recently, window coverings were only considered decorations. Architects have finally come to the realization that window coverings are the critical "third leg" of a dynamic facade tripod that is needed to ensure building comfort and efficiency. For the building design to function correctly, window coverings must be elevated in the design scheme to a critical system on par with HVAC and lighting.

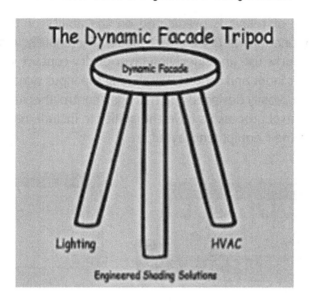

Integration Methodology

There are two main strategies used to integrate a shade motor network into an automated building system. The first is software control via hardware bridging. The second is software control via a software bridge. Both systems are perfectly acceptable, but they have very different designs and implementation structures.

Software Control via Hardware Bridge

This method of integration has some particular advantages. A well-designed shading system will usually work with a tremendous amount of flexibility within the context of its own equipment and programming. It is reasonable to expect a building-management controller to work well within its own hardware and programming sphere. In other words, we have two separate systems that function exactly as they were designed to.

Hardware bridging physically separates the two systems via the use of relays as the connection bridge. This configuration uses the relay bridge as an operational and diagnostic firewall and assists in delineating responsibility when malfunctions occur.

The use of relays is predicated on the ability of the shading system to function via dry contact inputs. Fortunately, most shade motor networks use an underlying layer of dry contact switches to manage user input and control. Paralleling the input signals via relay closures is an easily designed and managed control mechanism. Most building control processors have the ability to include relay-contact closures in their equipment layout.

Software Control via Software Bridge

This method offers the highest degree of systems integration, allowing the individual systems to become one. While technologically superior, experience has shown that the inclusion of shading motors into this control scheme is fraught with myriad problems. It's not that the concept is flawed, but the available equipment and expertise required are often not up to the task.

The concept is predicated on a common network protocol, such as BACnet or KNX, using a hardwired RS-232/422/485 backbone to distribute the control signals. To achieve success on high-end systems, which include hardware and software, engineering must be done from the ground up. Using a purely software approach for shade motor integration is highly dependent on engineers being proficient in custom software programming along with properly designed equipment. Designing and implementing the software can be an expensive layer of cost in project budgeting.

Software-Controlled Shading Systems

One of the newest trends in shade control is the use of digital networks to handle all the shades' functional requirements. On paper, these networks offer the advantages of sleeker layouts and functionality for the end user. Built around an RS-485 backbone, manufacturers claim that hundreds of motors can be controlled over distances up to four thousand feet with an overlay of intelligent software control.

The concept is simple. The motors are continuously powered with 120 or 24 volts, and Cat-5 cable distributes the control signals along the network to control all the motors. Each shade motor has its own digital address and can respond in myriad ways, depending on the discrete commands issued to it by the network controllers. When combined with digital switches, timers, sun sensors, wind sensors, and control algorithms, a truly intelligent shading system becomes a reality.

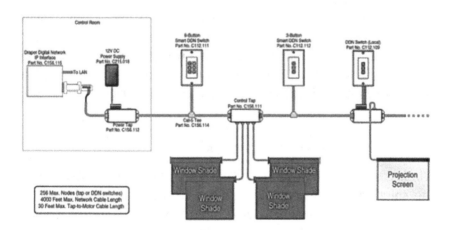

High-Voltage External Motor Controllers

From a pure reliability point of view, the tried-and-true external motor control systems are tough to beat. They may not be technically superior, but they will work in the field for decades with little or no problems. They offer limited intermediate stopping positions, which are approximated by motor runtime to a programmed stopping position. Many end-users usually only have the need for up-stop-down controls and do not need an expensive control overlay.

They are very wire dependent as well as structured in their layout. Centralized control location is very easy to diagnose and repair. Programming is clunky but easy to manage, and some manufacturers have placed well-designed graphical user interfaces (GUIs) on top of the controllers to modernize the programming process. The downside to this configuration is wiring cost and equipment space allocation, and expanding these systems can be problematic.

Low-Voltage Motors with Internal Control Logic

Because low-voltage motors use twelve or twenty-four volts, wiring is greatly simplified. Clients asking for expensive motorization usually do not want—and will not tolerate—high-voltage wiring that hangs from the shades and is plugged into a wall outlet.

The only downside is the needed addition of 24-volt power supplies, which can be a costly offset to the low-voltage wiring savings. There is also the torque limitation on low-voltage motors that make them incompatible with projects requiring large or coupled shade units. The use of high-performance, lightweight shade cloths can mitigate some of these limitations.

Radio Frequency Wireless Control (RF)

Wireless control in both high- and low-voltage versions is unanimously the solution for small-to-medium-sized projects. Considering the pros and cons of various power solutions, the wireless control scheme is a clear and decisive winner for many projects.

Grouping and intermediate stopping positions are part of the handheld remote control overlay, along with timers and sun sensors as upgrades. Expansion is simple, and many end users with minimal training can handle changing the control configuration.

The downside is that wireless control may not always work reliably in RF-rich environments, multiple-dwelling units, hospitals, correctional facilities, and secure government and private facilities where absolute control over the shading system is paramount.

Digital Network Control

Digital motor networks are the technology champions with vast control options. Wiring is minimized, and software can handle integration across a variety of systems. For the average project, this concept is complete overkill.

Finally, architects and owners should consider the proprietary nature of many of the control systems being offered. Proprietary does not translate into superior design and engineering. It is often a mechanism to protect the manufacturer's market share and enhance the profits delivered to its dealer network. Systems with more open control topographies usually are the budget winners on most projects.

Interview with Somfy Systems Experts

Somfy Systems is the world leader in motorization and automation for the window-covering industry. They manufacture motors and intelligent systems for all types of blinds, shades, awnings, and rolling shutters. Since motorization and automation are the driving force in engineered shading systems, it only makes sense to include such important content. My interview is with two of Somfy's leading individuals with architectural and engineering experience: Russell Horowitz, the architectural specification manager in the Northeast, and Ty Saville, the architectural/engineering market specifications manager.

NG: How did Somfy get involved selling shade motors?

TS & RH: Somfy began in 1750 in a French valley that borders Switzerland, manufacturing parts for Swiss watches. This region is where the Somfy name originates. Somfy is an acronym; it stands for Societe d'Outillage Mecanique du Faucigny, which translates to Mechanical Tooling Company of Faucigny. By 1868, the company had expanded and now manufactured a wide range of products and components, including fishing reels and rods. In 1969, a local awning and shutter manufacturer contacted various companies in the area looking for a solution to power their products. Somfy was the only company able to manufacture a prototype. This was the first step in a whole new direction for the company.

In 1977, Somfy expanded to the United States. Manually retractable awnings were commonplace, so motorization was a welcomed feature. Motorized projection screens and interior shades quickly followed. Somfy first touched on home automation in 1981 with the launch of the "Somfy-matic," the first weather-controlled awning and shutters, capable of sensing weather conditions and automatically adjusting awnings and shutters appropriately. Today, we are helping to create smart homes and workplaces. Smartphones or tablets can remotely control Somfy products; additionally, our products integrate into popular home automation systems, including Crestron, Honeywell, and AT&T.

NG: What are the major automation strategies that Somfy focuses on?

TS & RH: Somfy is always looking at ways to expand the automation and motorization marketplace. To do this, we divide up the resources into residential and commercial, as there are different drivers in both markets. The Somfy residential team has been promoting the home-automation message in an effort to educate the end users on the benefits of automation within the home. This used to be out of reach for most consumers due to technology and cost limitations; with this information, Somfy has developed more intuitive, patented technology and looked at ways to be more price competitive. This has had a positive impact on reaching a larger number of consumers over recent years.

With the rapid growth in this industry, Somfy's main strategy is to continue working with the leading brands in automation to ensure seamless integration for our users. Somfy has interfaces that control automated shades; these are available in technologies such as RS232, RS485, BACnet, Z-Wave, ZigBee, or Wi-Fi. Somfy's Commercial Building Solutions offer a wide range of intelligent motors and controls, such as Animeo IP, that optimize the utilization of natural light in commercial workspaces.

Somfy's commercial specification team is LEED accredited and will support all aspects of any project, from specification through commissioning. From basic smartphone control to advanced automated building-management solutions, Somfy has a system to meet today's automation demands.

NG: How does Somfy systems provide solutions for LEED?

TS & RH: Somfy Systems is a member of the USGBC and is proud to offer our solutions to earn LEED credits. Somfy solutions for building automation of shading and natural ventilation devices create a bioclimatic facade. By interacting with outside elements to best utilize natural light and air while providing thermal and visual comfort, Somfy solutions contribute to energy savings, occupant comfort, and design innovation.

Somfy solutions have a high impact on the available points attributed to daylighting (Indoor Environmental Quality Credit 7— up to three points available) a certain percentage of the building. There are many other points available related to automated window coverings, but they would need to work in conjunction with the lighting and HVAC system within the building. Some potential points include light-pollution reduction (Sustainable Sites Credit 6—one point available), thermal comfort of occupants (Indoor Environmental Quality Credit 5—one point available), and providing quality views (Indoor Environmental Quality Credit 8—up to two points available).

Somfy has the ability to contribute to the optimization of the energy performance within the entire building by influencing how the building envelope interacts with the environment. Due to points being delivered against energy-saving percentage, all systems within the building must work in unison to achieve the available eighteen points (Energy & Atmosphere Credit 2—eighteen points available against 50 percent energy savings).

The overall LEED objective is to achieve a truly holistic approach in building design to ensure all systems will work together to reduce the energy footprint and increase occupant comfort. Automated window coverings powered by Somfy have the ability to provide

LEED points necessary to help projects achieve Certified, Silver, Gold, or Platinum status.

NG: What is the future for Somfy products as architects focus on sustainable buildings?

TS & RH: Somfy's focus on developing innovative products that promote more energy-efficient buildings started many years ago with the Somfy-matic and continues today with Animeo IP. Our systems are calibrated to maximize occupant comfort while enhancing the visual environment, minimizing solar glare and heat gain, and providing UV protection. Somfy's natural light control and automation systems are scalable in design, offered in low-voltage, line-voltage, or wireless options, and are perfect for projects of any size or budget. This continued approach has kept Somfy solidified as the leader in the automated window-treatment market. As this market has evolved, Somfy has improved the tools available to its customers to help solidify their position with their clients. This includes partnerships with companies such as Integrated Environmental Studies (IES) who provide integrated, three-dimensional energy models that document the energy-load reduction on a building. These models allow for building owners and decision makers to compare energy performance results of using different types of glass with Somfy automated sun-shading devices, thus allowing the ability to make the correct choice for the building in question.

Somfy's focus on sustainable buildings is highlighted with the release of Animeo IP. Animeo IP is a total solar-management system utilizing Somfy-powered, intelligent motorized window coverings as well as digital keypads and weather sensors. The system's controllers, sensors, and keypads can be added to both new and existing Somfy Digital Network installations for comprehensive solar management as either a stand-alone solution or integrated into third-party control systems.

An intuitive user interface allows for simplified commissioning, building management, and technical support, featuring drag-and-drop programming, motor-auto discovery, and at-a-glance real-time system status updates. Animeo IP automatically manages motorized window coverings that reduce the dependency on artificial light, allowing more natural light for increased visual comfort of occupants, and energy savings.

Automated motorized window coverings are raised and lowered according to changes in outdoor weather conditions and indoor comfort needs based on commands from sensors, preprogrammed settings, or local-occupant controls. The Animeo IP's solar-tracking function is automated to ensure the reality of energy savings; 62 percent of energy use in commercial buildings is attributed to lighting and HVAC systems (USEIA 2003), which drives decision makers to increase energy efficiency with automation of critical systems such as facade management.

Chapter 15

Architectural and Contractor Services

Architectural Services

All of the solutions I've described are included in the toolbox that architects have at their disposal when working on residential, commercial, educational, government, or hospitality projects. What's missing is the expert advice from an engineered shading solution consultant. When architects work with consultants during the planning and design stages, products are proposed and integrated into the project as "engineered solutions" and not as afterthoughts. Consultants provide architects with many useful services in designing, planning, and fabricating engineered shading solutions.

Concept Drawings and Renderings

Concept drawing may be needed when a visual representation is required. The consultant may offer solutions from the toolkit of products, but sometimes there is a need for unique customization. The first step would be to provide a concept drawing like the one shown below. In this instance, the architect was seeking a treatment that would travel down a solarium skylight onto the vertical wall in one application.

On request, the consultant is also able to provide a computer rendering. The rendering below shows a concept for an exterior shading solution.

Computer Rendering

Mock-Ups

A mock-up is an actual working model that tests the capabilities of the architect's concept. For such a "never-been-done-before" solution, a mock-up is recommended. Engineered shading solutions are not a "cross-your-fingers-hope-it-works" endeavor. These solutions must be tested and guaranteed to function correctly. The best way to do that is with a fully functioning mock-up.

Three-Part Specifications

If required, the consultant should provide the architect with the properly executed three-part specifications. Engineered shading solutions mostly fall into the Master Format's Division 12 Furnishings category. However, exterior shading solutions are found in Division 10 Specialties (10 71 13).

Shade Mapping

Once the decisions are made concerning which solutions are to be specified on the project, the consultant provides the architect with a service called *shade mapping*. A shade map is a color-coded representation of the specified engineered shading solutions applied to the project plans.

The shade map includes the location of the shades on the floor plan and in elevation, the required wiring diagrams for the automated shades, the wood blocking for the installation of the brackets, and other pertinent details. When a shade map is provided to the general contractor, the architect knows that there are no excuses for costly mishaps such as inadequate electrical connections or missing wood blocking for the shades.

Contractor Services

It is unusual for architects to purchase the products they specify. The purchaser may be the owner or the owner's representative, which is the general contractor in most cases. For that reason, the consultant provides the following services to the contractor or owner.

Takeoffs

Plan takeoffs are a part of the cost-estimating process in the construction industry. Estimators use construction blueprints—either manually or electronically—and start "taking off" quantities of items they will need from those blueprints in order to prepare part of the estimate. In anticipation of requests by architects and contractors, the consultant will be asked to do a plan takeoff. This enables the consultant to study the project details and prepare an estimate.

Estimates

The consultant will prepare a detailed product cost that is based on the sizes provided by the plan takeoff. If the estimate is based on the plan takeoff, the prices are considered estimates only and are subject to field measurements for final pricing.

Submittals

Submittals in construction management are shop drawings, material data, samples, and product data. Submittals are required primarily for the architect and engineer to verify that the correct products and quantities will be installed on the project. The consultant is able to submit the necessary submittals as needed.

Installation

The consultant is able to provide or arrange for expert installation as detailed in the project's contract. The installation is critical to the success of any engineered shading solution. The installation service begins with field measurements.

During field measurements, the consultant records the exact dimensions and details for the fabrication of the engineered shading solution. It is also an opportunity to make sure the area for the installation is prepared properly. This includes correct pocket dimensions, necessary wood blocking, legal wiring details, and the avoidance or elimination of obstructions that would prevent the shade from functioning properly.

Project Management

Most projects require a key person to deal with the various parties involved. Since engineered shading solutions are an integrated part of the dynamic facade, there will be overlap with other trades. This may include all or some of the following: architect, contractor, electrician, audio/visual, carpenter, and owner. The consultant is able to perform as a project manager in order to coordinate the successful site preparation, installation, waivers of lien, and closeout documents.

Closeout Documents

Once a project is completed, the contractor may ask for documents to close out the job. This may include LEED documents, certified payroll reports, product warranties, attic stock, and product training. The consultant will assist in providing the necessary documents, certified payroll reports, attic stock, and product training.

Chapter 16

Architect's Challenge

The Architect's Challenge is a scenario presented by the architect to the engineered shading solution consultant. In this chapter, there are six scenarios that cover a range of specific solution sets: a single-family home, a hotel room, a large open office space, a corporate office building, a classroom, and a patient room. Each scenario offers a challenge to the consultant by the architect. The challenge consists of a wish list of solutions with specific outcomes for such things as reduction in solar heat gain, blocking the light from the window, reducing the cost of motorization, and daylighting without glare.

Single-Family Home

Architect's Challenge

The first challenge is a brownstone renovation located in the Prospect Park area of Brooklyn, New York. The Architect's Challenge is to provide a wireless shading solution throughout the brownstone. The windows in the living areas are to have shades that allow light to filter through but provide the client with complete privacy. The bedrooms require a dual solution of both a privacy weave and a blackout fabric. Also, the architect would prefer the shade rollers to be hidden in the ceiling.

Fabrics

The request for the fabric in the living room is to allow light to filter through but provide privacy. Most solar shade fabrics have an openness factor that ranges from 1 percent to more than 16 percent. Even a 1 percent fabric doesn't provide complete privacy, especially viewed from the outside in, at night with the interior lights on. Fortunately, there is a privacy weave that does exactly what the architect wants—light filtration through the fabric with total privacy.

The bedrooms require dual shades of both a privacy weave and a blackout fabric. The same privacy fabric specified for the living areas will work in the bedrooms. Since this is a high-end residential project, the blackout fabric must be quality. The best choice is a PVC-free, acrylic foamed-back fabric that gives a real cloth-like appearance.

Controls

The controls are requested to function as a wireless system. Since the windows are mostly single windows, low-voltage motors can be specified since high levels of torque are not required. The advantage of low-voltage motors is that the wiring can be done with data cables without the labor of an electrician. The controllers are five-channel wireless wall switches for each room. This provides flexibility in programming since the shades can be controlled individually or in groups with one wall switch.

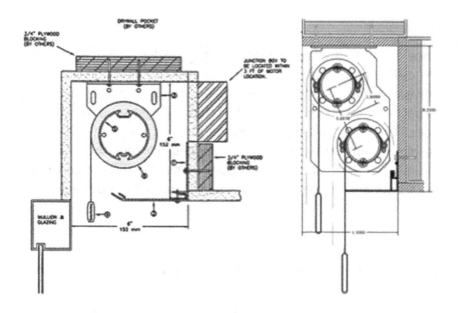

Installation

The architect's design is for the shades to be hidden in the ceiling. There are single shades in the living areas and dual shades in the bedrooms. The recessed pockets (shown above) with a closure plate can accommodate both. The pockets are also a good place to connect the power to the motors.

Hotel Room

Architect's Challenge

A new hotel needs blackout shades for all the guest rooms. The architect is requesting shades that allow no light seepage. The fabric must be fire retardant and controlled by a wall switch next to the bed. There is no room for a recessed pocket, so the shade roller needs to be enclosed below the ceiling line.

Hardware

Since the architect is specifying that the shades be mounted below the ceiling line, there must be a cassette to house the roller and prevent a light gap above the roller. Along with the aluminum cassette, sidetracks are required to stop any light seepage from the sides. The first challenge to address is a recurring issue of guests pushing against the fabric and dislodging it from the channels. Mounting the shades close to the glass eliminates this problem since the guests are unable to push the fabric out of the sidetracks.

Fabric

The best blackout fabric is a PVC-free, acrylic, foamed-back fabric that gives a real cloth-like appearance. The fabric is very durable for commercial use and has a fire classification of NFPA 701.

Controls

A robust control solution would be a line-voltage motor operated with a wired wall switch. This would be a single-pole, double-throw maintained switch. Maintained switches are required for a hotel room, and the motor will automatically stop when it reaches its set upper or lower limits.

Office

Architect's Challenge

The architect is requesting shades for its offices in New York City. The space is an entire floor with windows wrapping around on all four sides. The architect would like motorized solar shades but is not sure the budget will allow for such an expenditure. Employees working in front of southern and western exposures are complaining about glare and solar heat gain. The architect is also concerned that the shades will not be operated to filter the sun effectively because the staff is often out of the office on projects and doesn't pay much attention to the shades.

Fabric

The office space has windows on all four exposures. A good choice for a solar shade fabric would be one that comes in the same color in several degrees of openness. For the northern exposure, a 10 percent open would suffice, and 5 percent openness would be effective for the eastern-facing windows. For the southern and western openings, 3 percent is necessary.

Hardware

A big challenge is how to offer a motorized system on a budget. An effective solution to reduce the costs of motorization is with a technique called *coupling*. A coupling system allows one motor to drive multiple shades. This reduces the number of motors required as well as the electrical labor (see the photos above)

Controls

The architect's concern about the staff operating the shades at critical times of solar heat gain can be addressed by providing a timer. The shades can be programmed to raise or lower at certain times of day to help manage heat gain in the summer months and heat loss during the winter.

Architect's Challenge

The architect is working on a six-story office building in Miami, Florida. With a need to reduce solar heat gain, the best solution would be an exterior shading system. However, there is a concern about the durability of the shades due to the potential of high winds. The architect understands the effectiveness of an exterior shade in significantly reducing solar heat gain but is worried that the staff will not properly control the shades to maximize this benefit.

Exterior Shading Solution

The gravity-assisted exterior shading solution (shown above) is a motorized system with an elegantly designed tubular cassette. The aluminum housing protects the roller shade components from the elements. The shade has a telescopic bottom bar that slides along the stainless steel side cables. The cassette and cable brackets are designed to integrate with the facade.

Fabric

Since this project is located in a tropical climate, the fabric needs to provide excellent performance. The exterior shade fabric with a 3 percent openness factor will block out more than 85 percent of solar heat gain.

Wind Sensor

A wind sensor is required for any exterior shading solution. The sensor will automatically raise the shade when the sensor registers a programmed level of wind gust.

Sun Tracking

Since the architect is concerned that the staff will not operate the shades as required, sun-tracking software is needed. The exterior shades are equipped with sun sensors that position the shades at predetermined stops at the window. As the angle of the sun changes, the shades are programmed to stop at intervals based on the time of day and year as well as the geographical location.

Patient Rooms

Architect's Challenge

This project is for twenty-four intensive care rooms in a hospital in Manhattan. The rooms are in constant use and need a Dual Shading Solution (solar shade and blackout). The challenges are the need for individual patient control for the shades and control at the nurses' station for each room. There is also a space issue; the typical dual shade configuration of a blackout shade installed over the solar shade will not fit in a five-inch-tall pocket.

Fabric

The fabrics for a health care facility need to be fire retardant and antibacterial. The solar shade fabric in a 5 percent open will allow the patient to have a filtered view of the outdoors, and the blackout option will allow the patient to make the room dark during the daytime.

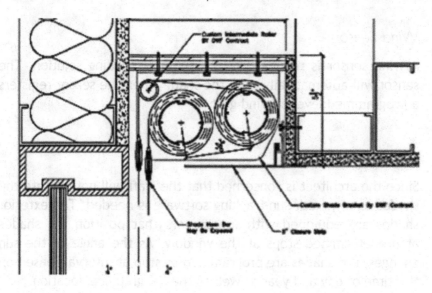

Hardware

The big challenge for the architect is to mount a dual shading solution into a five-inch-tall pocket. One option is to mount the shades side by side with the blackout shade closer to the glass. However, this is a clumsy solution since the solar shade fabric would be very far from the glass. The solution (shown above) answers this challenge with a bracket assembly that incorporates a secondary roller for the blackout fabric to snake up around the solar fabric and land close to the glass.

Controls

The controls for this system will be suitable for low-voltage systems with hardwired wall switches at the nurses' station and integration with the handheld patient controller at the bedside.

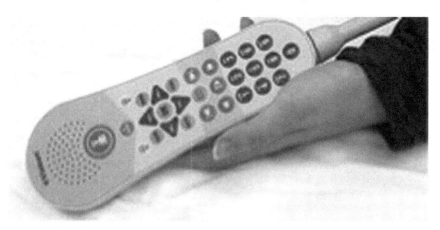

Patient Room Controller

Patient Room Controller

Chapter 17

Dynamic Projects

Interior Shading Solution

Project: Central kitchen, Englewood New Jersey

Engineered Shading Solution: To reduce solar heat gain and glare

Product: Interior shading solution with bullnose cassette

Fabric: Metallized 5 percent open fabric

Controls: Manual spring-assist clutch

Skylight Shading Solution

Project: Residence, New York City

Engineered Shading Solution: Reduce solar heat gain and light

Product: Tensioned Zip Skylight

Fabric: 5 percent Mesh Fabric

Controls: Line voltage with integrated controls

Blackout Shading Solution

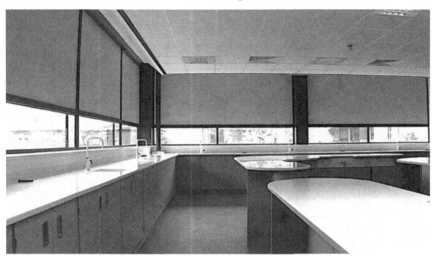

Project: Master bedroom, Scarsdale, New York

Engineered Shading Solution: Eliminate light into bedroom

Product: Blackout Zip shade

Fabric: Blackout shade fabric

Controls: Low-voltage wireless controls

Zip Light Block Solution

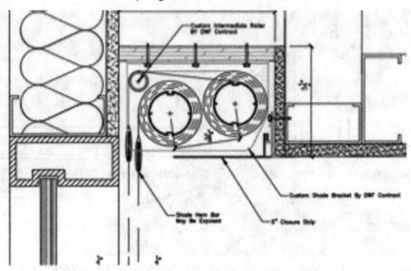

Project: Science building, West Point Military Academy

Engineered Shading Solution: To provide two levels of light control

Product: Dual Shading Solution within
recessed pocket with redirect roller

Fabric: 5 percent openness solar shade and blackout shades

Controls: Motorized with wired switches

Exterior Shading Solution

Project: Vancouver Olympic Village, Vancouver, Edmonton

Engineered Shading Solution: To reduce solar
heat gain for radiant HVAC system

Product: Exterior cable-guided shading solution

Fabric: 14 percent openness exterior solar shade fabric

Controls: Automated system with sun and wind sensors

Project: Aufgang Architects Building, Suffern, New York

Engineered Shading Solution: To reduce solar heat gain and glare

Product: Exterior cable-guided shading solution

Fabric: 14 percent openness exterior solar shade fabric

Controls: Automated system with sun and wind sensors

Chapter 18

Four Myths about Exterior Shades

As I present my Lunch and Learn program—Exterior Shading Solutions: The Next Generation in Window Coverings—to architects, designers, and consultants across the United States, I find myself addressing some similar misconceptions about this new trend in window shades. The four most common myths about exterior shading solutions are:

1) These shades cannot survive bad weather conditions.
2) They must have a short life span.
3) Maintenance must be a problem.
4) Interior shades cost less than exterior shading solutions.

Before I address these myths individually, it is important to understand that exterior shading solutions are becoming a significant part of many growing trends in architecture. For example, the passive-house movement has been gaining popularity in the United States. With the requirements of the passive house to reduce energy costs by 90 percent over a traditionally constructed home, exterior shading solutions are becoming an integral part of passive-house design.

As a functioning element on the building facade, exterior shading solutions are considered a part of *kinetic architecture*. Kinetic architecture is a concept through which buildings are designed to allow parts of the structure to move without reducing overall structural integrity. Kinetic architecture is becoming a force in sustainable building across the globe and is a significant contributor to a growing trend in exterior window shades. If these shades are to be successful as moving part of a structure, they must be reliable and robust. With that said, let's examine the four most common myths about exterior shading solutions

Stormy Weather

High Winds

The number one concern I encounter is the issue with high winds. Yes, high winds could be a problem if an exterior shading solution is not retracted before the high wind event occurs. That is why all exterior shading solutions are installed with wind sensors. For example, the cable-guided FM41 exterior shading solution calls for the wind sensor to send a signal to its motor to retract when wind gusts reach thirty-five miles per hour. To give you an idea of how often that may occur, thirty-five miles per hour is how a tropical depression is categorized. Between thirty-nine and seventy-three miles per hour is a tropical storm, and above seventy-four miles per hour is a hurricane-force wind. These wind conditions occur less than most people realize, but when there is a strong wind event, exterior shading solutions are retracted to a closed position and protected.

Rain, Snow, and Ice

Rain with winds below thirty-five miles per hour will cause no issue for an exterior shading solution. However, it is recommended that shades or blinds are retracted during harsh winter days with snow and ice. Snow and ice can prevent exterior shading solutions from functioning properly. Additionally, it is beneficial to have the exterior shading solution retracted because solar heat gain entering the space during wintertime is beneficial in reducing heating costs.

Life Expectancy

As an exterior product, our exterior shading solutions are manufactured to withstand the elements and have a long life expectancy. Let's break down the components:

Aluminum Extrusions: All the enclosures are extruded in aluminum and are extremely durable and long-lasting. Additionally, aluminum has a very high resistance to corrosion.

Motors: Line-voltage shade motors have, over the past twenty-five years, proven to be very reliable and robust. We have removed old shades where the fabric has worn out but the motor is still working without any issues. Today's basic line-voltage motors are only warrantied for five years but have the potential to last a quarter century or more without question.

Fabrics: The major manufacturer of fabrics for exterior shading solutions is Serge Ferrari. They serve the fabric architecture community throughout the world with amazingly durable, long-lasting fabrics. Their proprietary technology, Precontraint, creates a fabric that won't tear or stretch and is used on retractable roofs in stadiums worldwide. Our exterior shading solutions use the same fabrics.

Maintenance

Anything on the facade of a building needs some type of periodic maintenance. This is also true for exterior shading solutions. However, in the planning of these systems, we intentionally design them with the lowest-maintenance parts on the exterior. Let's examine these external elements:

Aluminum Extrusions: There is no maintenance required for any of the aluminum extrusions except an occasional washing, which can be carefully done with a pressure washer. You do not want to spray under the enclosure that protects the roller, motor, and power connections.

Cables: The six-millimeter cables need to be checked for tension occasionally.

Motors: The motor is the only part that may ever need to be replaced. The motor is located in the shade roller tube and is easily repaired.

Fabrics: The only maintenance ever needed on the fabrics is an occasional cleaning with a power washer.

Costs

This myth is my favorite to debunk. There is a wide-held belief that exterior shading solutions cost more than interior shades. This is not the case! Let's look at a price comparison between an interior and an exterior shade. Both shades are motorized and use basic fabrics.

Interior Solar Shade: Motorized 100 x 100 with an aluminum enclosure. Cost without installation: $1,125

Exterior Solar Shade: Motorized 100 x 100 with an aluminum enclosure. Cost without installation: $1,290

As you can see, the price of the exterior shade is slightly more than the comparable interior shade. The point is that if you are planning to do a motorized shade anyway, why not put it on the exterior where you can receive three times better performance and payback than with an interior shade.

Conclusion

The bottom line is that exterior shading solutions have been designed to deal with bad weather effectively and safely, have a long lifetime in service if they are maintained properly, and cost no more than interior shades. The benefits include tremendous reductions on solar heat gain and three times faster payback than interior shades.

Chapter 19

Final Thoughts

There have been great strides in the window-covering industry over the past several decades. Window coverings are no longer an afterthought, and they are now considered an integrated solution into the dynamic facade, along with lighting and HVAC. Local municipalities require new structures to meet high-performance building standards. This means new construction must be energy efficient through sustainable ideas, and window coverings are playing a major role. These new demands have required the maturation of window coverings into engineered shading solutions.

There are many innovations coming from designers, manufacturers, and fabricators of these systems. Some of the most interesting solutions are coming from Europe, where energy efficiency is highly valued. These engineered shading solutions are just now hitting our shores.

All throughout Europe, exterior shading solutions have been installed for years with great results. Realizing the benefits of both sustainability and aesthetics, architects in the United States are slowly starting to specify exterior shading solutions for projects.

It is my hope that engineered shading solutions will continue to grow and provide effective control of solar heat gain, glare, and light to benefit the occupants in residential, commercial, educational, hospitality, and government applications.

We will see amazing innovations over the coming years and decades. Some are already available, and others are in development.

Here are a few inspirational solutions on my radar and on my wish list:

- dynamic glass that changes opacity on demand
- photovoltaic exterior roller shades that produce energy
- biomimetic-inspired solutions in fabrics that open and close the weave like an eye's iris

On the second point of photovoltaic exterior roller shades to produce energy, I interviewed Robert Lerner of Pvilion. Pvilion designs and manufactures flexible photovoltaic solar structures and products, ranging from solar-powered charging stations to solar-powered curtains, building facades, and clothing.

Interview with Robert Lerner of Pvilion

Over the past few years, solar power has been growing exponentially. Some of the factors behind the surge in popularity has been the US Government Investment Tax Credit for Renewable Energy, the Obama administration's pro-solar policies, and the increasing technological advances across a wide spectrum, which have brought the costs down significantly enough to compete with mainstream energy sources like coal.

Recently, Tesla Energy announced a battery-storage system for both residential and commercial applications. This is big news for the future of the solar power industry since there are feasible, cost-effective ways to store solar-power-generated electricity for sunless days.

Research is being done across myriad solar power solutions. My company, InSync Solar, has teamed up with photovoltaic experts at Pvilion. Pvilion's expertise is in the integration of all steps along the process. InSync Solar and Pvilion are developing the first exterior solar shade that reduces solar heat gain and generates electricity with a flexible, photovoltaic shade cloth. In other words, we are putting the "solar" into solar shades. Below is my interview with Robert Lerner, one of the principals at Pvilion.

NG: What does Pvilion do?

RL: Pvilion is a design, engineering, and manufacturing company, which specializes in integrating flexible photovoltaic into architectural projects and mass-produced products. We got a start about twenty years ago when we designed and manufactured the first photovoltaic tent. Since then, we've developed the first military shelters that had solar panels integrated into the skins, and we've designed and installed custom architecture solar structures for some very notable landmark projects. We work on projects at large and small scales, from designing solar jackets for Tommy Hilfiger to fabricating major buildings as part of a team of architects, engineers, and manufacturers.

NG: How did Pvilion get started?

RL: Pvilion is a third-generation company that has its origins in the late 1970s. Todd Dalland founded FTL Design Engineering, a design-engineering firm that specialized in lightweight membrane structures. After changing the world of tensile-structure architecture, Todd Dalland and I spun off a new company called FTL Solar in 2005. FTL Solar sought to commercialize the research and development into solar-technology integration with a proprietary set of products, mainly targeting the military market.

In 2011, Todd Dalland, Colin Touhey, and I founded Pvilion as an independent spin off from FTL Solar to focus on architectural and commercial product lines, also utilizing the base technology of flexible photovoltaic and lightweight building materials. Some notable projects came about rather soon: the Solar Sail in Pflugerville, Texas, utilized flexible photovoltaic on thin sheets of twisted stainless steel. This patent-pending technology has since been used on another product we call the Solar Trellis. Pvilion now has architectural projects in development worldwide and is working with InSync Solar to develop operable PV shading systems for the exterior of buildings.

NG: How does Pvilion envision the PV industry in the next five years?

RL: We see further adoption of PV technology as an alternative energy source. We also see increasing globalization of the module and cell industries. However, we see more opportunity for manufacturing to come back to the United States. For example, we recently completed some projects in which the cells were manufactured in Taiwan, turned into modules in Europe, then shipped to us in Brooklyn, where we converted them to finished products, and then shipped out to customers in California or even Europe. Of course, this is unique for the solar industry at large, but we may see more of this happening as the appetite for more interesting solar projects increases. It used to be that solar was thought of categorically in terms of "how can I install the greatest number of panels at the lowest cost to give me the quickest return on investment." Now PV is poised to become another architectural piece of a building that is thought of in terms of esthetics, functionality, and return on investment.

NG: What is your vision for incorporating exterior shades and photovoltaic?

RL: The beauty of the exterior shade photovoltaic system is that it combines active and passive benefits of shading and power generation. Shading reduces the cooling load on the building while reducing glare and increasing comfort. Exterior shades offer large surface areas, which can also be generating photovoltaic energy. These large surface areas on the elevations of the buildings are a significant untapped solar resource. Our vision is to make these operable photovoltaic shades a beautiful architectural enhancement to the facade. Facades of buildings will be more dynamic, changing with the weather and the time of day. Solar panels will be produced with color choices, so they won't all look alike.

NG: What are the advantages of a photovoltaic-exterior shade over panels installed on the roof?

RL: Very often the roof of a building is encumbered by mechanical equipment that uses up valuable real estate and which would also shade a photovoltaic array. Additionally, rooftop installations sometimes require roof penetrations or ballasts that are heavy. We see the photovoltaic-exterior shade system as something that might be done in addition to a rooftop installation or in lieu of a rooftop installation. The main advantage, however, is that the photovoltaic exterior shade system performs two functions at once. It reduces cooling load and provides power. Once a customer decides to install operable shades, the marginal cost increase of adding solar to the shade will be worth it since there wouldn't be any additional structural costs.

Conclusion

Window coverings and exterior shading solutions have evolved into an important sustainable building system. Exterior shades and blinds reduce solar heat gain by more than 85 percent and soon will produce renewable energy. We are about to put "solar" into solar shades.

Glossary

blackout shade. A blackout shade is a shading solution that allows no light to pass through the fabric. Light seepage around the sides and top are eliminated with a cassette and sidetracks.

bottom-up shade. When the shade pulls up from the bottom of the window to the top.

cassettes. Cassettes are an aluminum housing for the shade roller, fabric, brackets, and controls for both manual and motorized shades.

closeout documents. Once a project is completed, the contractor may ask for documents to close out the job. These may include LEED documents, certified payroll reports, product warranties, attic stock, and product training.

coupled shades. Coupling is a strategy to link several shades together with one 120-volt motor. This reduces the number of motors and switches needed to control large window areas and eliminates the need for additional wiring and outlets.

daylighting. Daylighting is the practice of placing windows or other openings and reflective surfaces so that natural light provides effective internal lighting during the day.

dual shades. Dual Shading Solutions combine a solar shade and a blackout shade in the same opening, providing a wide range of light control.

engineered. Engineered is a creative application of scientific principles to design and develop structures with respect to their intended functions.

engineered shading solutions. Engineered shading solutions are sustainable systems for interior and exterior window coverings that engage the latest technologies to control heat, glare, and light.

exterior shades. Exterior shading solutions are roller shades, tensioned shades, or horizontal louvers mounted on the exterior of windows. Exterior shading solutions provide greater performance in reducing solar heat gain than interior solutions do.

glare. Glare is a visual sensation caused by excessive and uncontrolled brightness.

group control. Multiple shades in multiple areas are programmed to respond together from one switch (for example, all the shades on the south side of the building).

ISO relays. To function multiple shades off one wall switch requires an ISO relay. ISO relays are used to make this happen while concurrently protecting the motors from the destructive electrical feedback caused by collapsing magnetic fields generated when the motors are suddenly turned off by their limit switches.

light pollution. Light pollution is excessive, misdirected, or obtrusive artificial light.

limit switch. A limit switch is a switch that prevents the travel of an object in a mechanism past some predetermined point, mechanically operated by the motion of the object itself.

local control. Each shade is controlled individually or within the context of small, localized groups by one switch (for example, all the shades in a particular office or room).

maintained switches. A switch that physically keeps the button and circuit in the actuated position (open or closed). In other words, when the key or push switch is actuated, it stays in the on or off position until actuated again.

manual controls. An engineered shading solution that is controlled by a device that functions the solution without motorization.

master control. All the shades in the project are programmed to respond to one switch (for example, to raise all the shades for window cleaning or lower them for security at the end of the workday).

mock-up. In manufacturing and design, a mock-up is a scale or full-sized model of a design used for evaluation purposes. A mock-up is a prototype that provides at least part of the functionality of a system and enables testing of a design.

momentary switches. A type of switch (usually in the form of a push button) that is only engaged while it is being depressed (as opposed to a typical on/off switch that latches in its set position).

motorized engineered shading solution. An engineered shading solution that functions with a tubular motor with wired or wireless controls with line or low-voltage power.

newton meters. The newton meter is a unit of torque in the SI system. The symbolic form is Nm or N.m. One newton meter is equal to the torque resulting from a force of one newton applied perpendicularly to a moment arm, which is one meter long.

noise reduction coefficient. The noise reduction coefficient (NRC) is a scalar representation of the amount of sound energy absorbed upon striking a particular surface. An NRC of zero indicates perfect reflection, and an NRC of one indicates perfect absorption.

photovoltaic. Photovoltaic (PV) is the name of a method of convertingsolar energy into direct current electricity using semiconducting materials that exhibit the photovoltaic effect, a phenomenon commonly studied in physics, photochemistry, and electrochemistry.

radio control. Control of an apparatus from a distance by means of signals transmitted from a radio or electronic device.

recycled content. Recycled content refers to the portion of materials used in a product that has been diverted from the solid waste stream. If those materials are diverted during the manufacturing process, they are referred to as *preconsumer recycled content.*

regular and reverse roll. Regular roll is when the fabric rolls off the back of the roller. Reverse roll is when the fabric rolls off the front of the roller, leaving more space between the shade fabric and the glass.

shade mapping. Shade mapping provides extensive detail of where each type of shade is located directly on the architectural plans. It is a color-coded visualization that provides complete details.

shading solutions. Shading solutions refers to the answers to common issues and problems caused by too much solar heat gain, glare, and light.

sidetracks. Sidetracks are aluminum extrusions that support the movement of the bottom rail for skylight and bottom-up solutions as well as fabric to be inserted for the purposes of providing complete blackout.

smart-device control. The latest trend in window-covering control is the use of smart devices to directly control shading systems (systems include ZigBee, Wi-Fi, Bluetooth, and Z Wave).

solar heat gain. Solar gain refers to the increase in temperature in a space, object, or structure that results from solar radiation. The amount of solar gain increases with the strength of the sun and with the ability of any intervening material to transmit or resist the radiation.

spring assist. A manual lifting device with a spring coil to lessen the load of force in lifting the engineered shading solution.

submittals. Submittals in construction management are shop drawings, material data, samples, and product data. Submittals are required primarily for the architect and engineer to verify that the correct products and quantities will be installed on the project.

sustainable design. Sustainable design is a collaborative process that involves thinking ecologically and studying systems, relationships, and interactions in order to design in ways that remove rather than contribute stress from systems.

takeoffs. Plan takeoffs are a part of the cost-estimating process in the construction industry. Estimators use construction blueprints, either manually or electronically, and start "taking off" quantities of items they will need from those blueprints in order to prepare part of the estimate.

velarium. The velarium was the Latin name given for the retractable awning system of the Roman Colosseum.

Zip shade. The Zip shade is manufactured with a zipper-like detail welded to the vertical edges of the fabric. These zippers run in tracks on each side and prevent the fabric from being pushed out of the aluminum side channels.

About the Author

Neil Gordon is the founder of InSync Solar, LLC, and Decorating with Fabric, Inc. Neil is an educator and provider of engineered shading solutions to the architectural community throughout the United States. As a thirty-year veteran in the window-covering industry, Neil works with designers, architects, and contractors to provide all types of window-covering solutions for residential, commercial, educational, hospitality, and governmental projects.

Index

147

Printed in the United States
By Bookmasters